EL PASO'S DARKEST DAY

Al Hernandez

EL PASO'S DARKEST DAY

First Printing/Publishing, 2020

ISBN: 979-862-1585-105

Albhernandez Publishing

EL PASO, TEXAS

United States of America

To my sister **Maribel's** loving memory.

May your soul rest eternally with your King at the top of the mountain.

(July 25,1963-August 3,2019)

Preface

In an ever-changing world where mass shootings have plagued the United States, a very dark pattern has emerged where victims die and are buried without a voice. I was inspired to write this book to give my sister the voice she no longer has. I hope to have represented, what I feel confident are, her views on gun violence and racial hate as accurately as possible. I wrote this because I couldn't accept that Maribel's death was in vain.

The story I've told is about what a family goes through when the unimaginable happens in their community. When a shooter walks into a place that you and all your loved ones frequent without any warning and just rips people from this world. When my sister was one of those people, I couldn't just let her go without showing the world who she was and how I knew her.

I want to tell my sister Maribel's life as it was before the shooting. I want to show what a victim of one of these shootings was doing all the way up to being shot with an AK-47. I want to show how the events that took place in the Walmart shooting had a huge ripple effect that not only touched the families involved, but the entire community. How ordinary people transform into heroes by making their final acts ones of valor so that others lived. How this repugnant act of domestic terrorism, targeting the Latino community specifically, didn't destroy us – it made us stronger.

I have read and watched so much coverage about the El Paso Walmart shooting that only spoke about the loss and the violence. This is a book about healing and how a community comes together in the strongest of ways to mend from a massively destructive situation caused by hate.

ACKNOWLEDGMENTS

I am so incredibly grateful to all the first responders who were largely responsible for many of the lives saved on August 3, 2019. Thank you for your prompt arrival at the scene and immediate call to action. Your quick apprehension of the attacker prevented his escape and ensured that he was unable to take any more innocent lives.

I would like to give a mention to the executive assistant to the mayor of El Paso, Ms. Winters. I greatly appreciate your prompt replies to my many inquiries and all your help in coordinating assistance for all the victims as well as their families after this tragic event.

I am very appreciative of my family who allowed me to write about them in, what I hope they found, the most flattering of ways. I love you all and thank God that you all are a part of my life.

Thank you, my editor, Juliet Leon Dewey, who did an amazing job in refining my words. Also, thanks to Debra Sanchez for finalizing the text and layout, to my book cover artist, Nick Caya, for your beautiful work. It looks amazing and you captured exactly what I envisioned.

To all the victims who were interviewed, I give an enormous thank you.

Table of Contents

Chapter 1

"I stand here at this podium at Austin High, looking out at the students. I never thought in a million years I'd be up here giving this type of speech. I didn't think there was going to be so many news media covering this ceremony honoring my sister, Maribel Hernandez."

The crowd in the stands looked down intensely at me. I stand here talking about a difficult topic that no one should have to be going through.

"Austin Panthers how are you guys doing today? Today we are here, not to talk about tragedy, but about life and healing."

***

My name is Al Hernandez. I've been a resident of the tranquil city of El Paso for several decades with my immediate, as well as my extended, family. We have enjoyed the serene calm of what has been the safest city I've ever known. El Paso was once such a small town that people could go any place and recognize friends or acquaintances. We've always been a very tight-knit and friendly community for as long as I can remember. Sunshine and good weather have kept my family here in El Paso. Before Khalid famed El

Paso as the "city of the 915" we were recognized and known as the "Amigo Sun City." That loosely translates to the Friendly Sun City.

El Paso is known as a border city, due to its proximity to the border of Ciudad Juarez, Mexico. This has contributed to El Paso having an overall Hispanic population of 83%, per the U.S. Census Bureau's webpage listed on March 30, 2020. The cities of El Paso and Juarez are interconnected: they share the Rio Grande, commerce, cultures, and family ties. Mexican nationals have always come to El Paso for shopping, to visit family members, or to have fun. At any given time, you can find a vast population of Juarez citizens in the El Paso area. These citizens are tourists that immensely contribute to the El Paso economy.

Juarez has many manufacturing plants from around the world, including Japan and the US. You can find executives and CEOs from many countries doing business in Juarez. Crossing the international bridge used to be smooth, and wait times were minimal. I remember when I was in elementary school, most of my teachers worked part-time as custom agents.

Juarez Boulevard was vibrant for many decades, and there was a slew of nightclubs that competed with the styles of LA and New York. High school students would fill the Juarez Boulevard on Friday and Saturday nights to go clubbing. In the early eighties, disco was big and El Pasoans flocked to Juarez in droves to party on the other side of the border. The Mexican Federales would keep Americans safe, and rarely did you hear of bad things happening. Maybe the occasional drunken brawl, but nothing crazy.

We frequently made trips to visit family on

my father's side. They lived in Juarez when it was safe and friendly. I remember my brothers, my sister, and I playing in a huge park by my grandmother's house. It was very safe. I could see that people left their doors open at night as we played in the park until nightfall. My sister, Maribel, whom we sometimes called Mary, loved to hang out at the park with our cousins, just talking or playing games.

On my mother's side we had, and still have, a huge number of relatives that have resided in Texas for generations. My grandfather was born in Marfa, Texas, which is a small farming community. My mother and my uncles were born in what was once the busy farming community of Fabens, Texas. My grandfather, Jose, was a farmer and rancher to his core. He was a tall, strong man who built his own house with his bare hands out of adobe with

14

no assistance. The house still stands today, and it looks just as strong and unwavering. Times were hard in those days, so my uncles had to leave their beloved small town to look for a better future. They found it in the U.S. military.

Eventually, all my uncles left at a young age to join different branches of the armed forces. Fort Bliss has always been an essential part of this region, and the US Army's veins run through the city. The presence of a military base has resulted in many people coming and going from all over the country. I've talked to so many soldiers throughout the years that have only fond recollections of their deployments at El Paso. I have always told people that are new to El Paso, "You'll know if you like it within the first few days."

Northeast El Paso has been a prominent

hub for many military families and retired Army veterans for generations. A strong Korean community grew and became established, as well as other cultural communities, due to the military presence.

Many members of my family fought in either World War II, the Korean War, or, in the case of our youngest relative to join the military – Domingo, the Vietnam War. After the wars ended, they migrated to various locales, primarily in California and Arizona, to build their own families. We never had a shortage of childhood friends with so many cousins to hang out with. We were self-branded the Bonilla Clan.

Mary and I were born and raised here in El Paso with our two brothers, Dave and Fred. Growing up we didn't have the Internet, cell phones, or Facebook, but we had a happy childhood. Maribel was a gorgeous girl who people often called "*Guera*," which is a Mexican-Spanish slang for a light-haired girl. Sometimes it means white girl, but in her case, it was about her long beautiful light brown hair and white complexion. Okay, she kind of looked like a white girl. She was Dad's little princess, and he adored her. He and my mother took shifts caring for her. During the day my father often took Maribel out to the park or shopping.

My father told us a story about how one day when he was at the Plaza, this lady sat across from him staring at him. It got awkward and after some time she confronted him. She told him, "Hey. I know that isn't your daughter. She's white."

My dad only laughed and called her, "Crazy woman," as he smiled. Then they got out of there.

My parents were kind and hardworking

individuals. My mother, Aurora, left the farming life to come and work for Farah Manufacturing. Willie Farah was the owner and today it is where the Fountains at Farah is located. She recalled him as a smart man with a big heart. She claimed you could often see supervisors riding on roller skates around the huge building. Our family had no shortage of stylish jeans and clothes due to my mother working there. She was always so proud that she worked in a company that took care of its employees.

Later the Chicanas, a Mexican American feminist group from another city, organized a strike that brought the company down. My mother was very upset and told us it was a huge mistake.

"He had transportation, nurses, gifts, bonuses. We had it made!" she would say.

My dad also worked in a garment

manufacturing plant. He learned multiple trades in his small farming town in Mexico.

He told us, "You have to show these hot-shot Gringos your skills."

When his bosses found out all the different jobs he could do they would page him over the intercom to come to their office. He'd have coffee with the big bosses. After they mingled a bit, they would take him to their cars and gave him as much time as he needed to do various repairs. Word got around town and he was bounced back and forth, from the factories fixing cars.

Other workers became jealous and would yell, "Hey Hector! You kiss ass! Get your ass over here and get to work!"

My dad later became good friends with a plant manager from Dallas, Bob Davis. They ended up being lifelong friends.

After many years of hard work, my parents

saved up enough money to buy a house. I remember vividly, cruising the Manhattan Heights area just looking for a home. My father saw a house he loved, primarily because it didn't require much yard work.

"Let's buy this one!" My dad shouted.

"No," my mother said. "We need a big yard for the kids." They continued up the mountain until my mother saw a small house with a big yard. We pulled up to the house and got out of the car. We all darted out. We were so sick of being stuck in the car. My mother saw us running around and playing in the yard all excited.

She told my dad, "Pay the man. This house is beautiful and it's mine!" I saw my father knock on the door and give, what I think was, the real estate guy or the homeowner a stack of bills – cash. That house became our childhood home.

Chapter 2

t was the 1970s, and the Vietnam War was still going on. Our new neighborhood was full of American flags. The neighborhood was very diverse. Mr. Bellamy was the neighbor who lived in the house directly in front of ours. He was a kind old man with frizzy white hair and a beautiful Dalmatian. To the right we had Mrs. Wilson, a retired teacher, who Maribel grew to love and continued to visit throughout her later years. Mrs. Wilson's husband had just died that year. He was a prominent El Paso firefighter. Mrs. Wilson had a huge German shepherd called King. King looked terrifying, but he was very gentle with all the kids. In the house to the left of us lived Margrett. She was a Mennonite woman that spoke fluent German and that had maintained all her motherland customs. Margrett was such a nice lady. She made the most delicious mulberry pies with fresh mulberries from a large mulberry tree in front of our home. She gave us free piano lessons and offered to teach us, German.

The Uribes moved into the home in front of our house later that year. They brought two girls with them, which my sister was thrilled about. Maribel had been the only girl since birth. She rode bikes, hiked, played softball, flew kites, and played with only boys all the time. She was sick of playing with just boys. Now there were two girls to join the gang: Pat and Julie. Almost everyone knew Maribel in the neighborhood, so she introduced the new girls to everyone. We were out and about until sundown. In those days we spent every waking moment outside until we had exhausted ourselves. Then we would eat and crash into bed.

My father was a very active man and took us hiking up the mountains weekly. On Saturdays, he took all four of us up the mountain through a cliffside trail.

Maribel clung to my dad's leg yelling, "Don't let me go, Apa!" My dad would grab her and swing her side-to-side smiling. She would giggle and laugh at the top of her lungs. It was hysterical.

"I got you, *Mija*. Don't worry!" my dad would reassure her. We grew to love the mountains and were nonstop climbers. We would walk up Scenic Drive just to watch the city from up high. You could see for miles on a cloudless day. We loved to go up to the edge of a peak on a clear, sunny day.

Sundays we took rides in my dad's 55 convertible Chevy. He'd fixed it up and was extremely proud of it. Our favorite thing to do was to ride, with the top down in the Chevy, all the way to the Plaza de Los Lagartos. They had real alligators wild and free in the downtown plaza! Maribel loved to throw popcorn at the alligators. No wonder it was named "Plaza de Los Lagartos" (Alligator Plaza). Those creatures owned that area.

Friday nights we used to go to the Bronco Drive-In and watch movies on the big screen. We loved hanging out at the snack bar, where they had swings and an endless supply of junk food. It was delicious.

My dad had Maribel spoiled when she was a little girl. There were two rooms in the basement that were right next to each other. Basements were quite common in old houses like ours, which we thought was cool. We all wanted to sleep there. But Maribel got a whole room for herself! Dave, Fred, and I had to share one room. Not fair! Maribel had lots of stuffed bears that we constantly wanted to play with. God forbid we ever got caught in her room, she would have beaten us up! She had her favorite teddy bear, Charlie, as the gatekeeper.

She told us, "Ask Charlie if you can come in first."

She ruled the downstairs. When she said, "Lights out!" – we turned the lights off. When she said, "TV off!" – we turned the TV off, unless we were watching wrestling. She loved to watch wrestling matches and sometimes tried out the techniques she learned on us! We couldn't say anything though because we could keep the TV on as long as there was wrestling on.

In our formative years, we attended Houston Elementary, which we walked to every morning. It was such an adventure to go to school, and come back from school, all by ourselves! We found there were a bunch of different ways to and from school that had us endlessly entertained. Maribel had us all split up and we'd race to see who would get home first. Fred and Maribel developed a strong bond and formed their team to pretty much win every time.

After school, it was fun times. We were independent children. Growing up in those days was so vastly different from today. We had a huge tube box TV where we'd watch our Sunday morning cartoons. We sat around reading comic books while my dad read novellas.

My parents had set up an account at the corner store, Los Alamos Grocery, which we could access so we could buy food after school if we got hungry. What we did was buy whatever we wanted on credit. We thought it was great! We made lots of friends since we offered to purchase snacks for everybody. When my parents went in to pay the account on payday, they wondered why the bill was so high.

They asked Old Jimmy, the store owner, "Do these kids eat that much?"

Jimmy just nodded his head, and said, "Yes." He was selling a lot of merchandise. Whether it was for our friends or not, he didn't care.

Back in those days, we had a few different babysitters for when my parents couldn't get home on time from work. You could hire a live-in babysitter from Ciudad Juarez for super cheap. Sometimes they were good sitters and sometimes they were bad ones. The bad ones weren't that bad they just weren't very friendly. Our cousin, Elena, was our favorite. She walked us to the park, and she was funny. We all learned how to cook at a very early age, thanks to her. We got good at cooking just by watching and helping her every day. Maribel made awesome enchiladas, Dave made handmade flour tortillas, and I made the best Mexican rice. As we got older, my parents figured out that we could cook. They expected us to prepare meals for them when they got home! From then on, we'd come home after school, watch our favorite shows, and afterward, we drew sticks to see who would cook what before our parents got home. Fred, who was the youngest, usually ended up cleaning the house. I don't know why we had him do it, but it probably had something to do with the fact that we hated doing it. He complained the whole time.

In the evenings we attended All Saints Catholic Church. My brothers and I became dedicated altar boys. As soon as we did, Maribel wanted to be an altar girl. When they told her that she wasn't allowed she had a full-on tantrum! She had to wait for us outside the church. After that, she waited patiently. The reason she waited is that Father Smith always paid us for doing his masses. She had a plan. Maribel then waited outside until we'd finished mass.

When we walked out, she'd grab us by the arm and say, "You guys got paid. Let's go! Take me to the store you bunch of clowns!"

One night after church my sister asked me, "Hey Beto. If you were ever to get lost, do you know what to do…especially at night?"

"No. Do you?"

"Yes! Of course, I do! Beto, if you ever get lost just look up at the mountains and you'll see those antennas. The first one on the left, you'll find our house right under it." Well, that information came in real handy later that year.

31

***

I was nine years old and hanging out with my church group after school. Our neighbor, Mrs. Uribe, was the organizer of the group and she had invited us all to go on a field trip to the circus. I realized I hadn't asked my parents, so I ran home and back to the church just as everyone was being counted to load up into two vans. I jumped right in! Mrs. Uribe asked me if my parents knew about the trip and I said, "Yes!" She nodded, so off we went.

The circus show was fabulous! I was with my group of buddies and having so much fun. I could see all the members of my church group were enjoying the circus too. As the finale for the performance ended, I saw the driver taking off outside.

"Oh no!" I thought and ran after him, so I'd be the first in the van. I pushed past a huge crowd, and when I got through, I'd lost the driver. I decided I should go out to the parking lot to find him there. I knew I could find the van when I got there since it was brand new. No problem. Well, when I got to the parking lot I panicked. All the vans were new and identical! I looked everywhere and I couldn't find the driver!

I heard Maribel's voice in my head, "If you ever get lost just look up at the mountains and you'll see those antennas. The first one on the left, you'll find our house right under it."

Well, I didn't know the actual distance too well, but I could see the antenna. I went for it. I began walking towards what I could see of one of the antennas. It was already getting dark. I walked and I walked and was gaining ground, but I didn't realize I was miles from home and now I was walking in the pitch, black night. I only had a short-sleeved t-shirt on, and the

33

temperature had dropped to what felt like freezing.

When they got back the church group realized they were short one kid. Mrs. Uribe went into a panic and her husband didn't know what he should tell my parents. When they finally mustered up the courage and called them, they were already freaking out because they didn't know where I was! Everyone was frantic!

"WHAT! You're telling me my child is lost and it's dark and no one can find him!" my mom shouted at them. My parents assembled several search teams of family and friends and began looking for me all over El Paso.

Meanwhile, I was walking, following the antenna that my sister had told me about. It was so cold and dark. The streets were empty. It must have been around eleven pm. I was walking in this dark neighborhood when a car pulled up next to me. The driver's side window lowered, and a man called to me to come over to him.

I did, and he asked, "Hey kid. What are you doing late at night walking here when it's so cold?" He lifted what I could barely see was a police badge. "I'm a detective." My shoulders dropped heavily in relief.

I told him my story and what Maribel said. "My sister told me that if I were ever to get lost, follow the antennas and underneath there would be my house."

He drove me to that area and said, "Okay kid. Tell me where your house is." We were right in the neighborhood, but I couldn't find my house.

After a while of driving around, he gave up and took me for a hamburger at Lucky's Cafe. The detective told the waitresses, "Hey, I just found this kid. Do any of you need a kid?" The ladies just smiled and giggled.

"Sure, we'll take him. Come on, *Mijo*," one said.

After we finished eating the detective took me to the police station and handed me to a uniformed officer. "See you kid," he said and waved goodbye.

I just stood there waiting. Then a nice older policeman walked up and said, "Hop in the car kid. I'm taking you home!"

He let me put on his police cap as we were driving up to my house. My parents saw the police car, with me in the front, and you could see the relief wash over their faces as they came out of our front door. My sister ran and hugged me. "You dummy! I was so scared you would not be found, *Pendejo*!" My sister and I eventually laughed about that story so much for years thereafter.

After that incident, All Saints Church became the only parent-approved hangout location. We could participate in on-site activities for the Catholic youth organization (CYO). If we ever wanted to go on a group trip again, I knew I needed to ask way ahead of time. We sold cupcakes on Sundays and eventually made enough money to go on a trip to the Western Playland Amusement Park, as well as to do skate night every Friday. Those were enjoyable times for us because we stayed out of trouble and made lots of friends. Father Smith let us use the church facility for our dancing parties. The dancing parties were where Maribel discovered boyfriends. All my friends had a crush on her, but she never liked any of them. She showed off her disco moves and in no time the boys thought they were *John Travoltas*, busting out the moves.

In the summers we developed a fun routine. We got up late, watched all our favorite programs, got ready, and took the bus downtown. The city had just replaced all the buses with brand new ones that had exquisite air conditioners. It was a cool ride. We then walked to Cathedral High and swam for hours. We became excellent swimmers. Maribel loved spending time with her friends. We stayed there all afternoon. Then we went to go buy food at the corner store and finally took the bus back.

Every summer we took a vacation. My parents loved to travel with the family. Our favorite places to visit were the Elephant Butte Lake and Caballo Lake. My father saved for a whole year so he could buy this boat that he even put a brand-new engine in.

He was so excited to tell us, "Now kids…we are going to camp out in style! A new engine to ride, like champs!"

On the Fourth of July, Dad hooked up the boat to the back of our truck and off we went to the Caballo Lake.

The moment we arrived at our destination, Dad dropped the boat in the water and took us all for a ride. After he'd been driving a while he pulled up to the dock.

He turned back and said, "I'm going to take a break. Take it for a ride but be careful." He jumped out and walked back to the campgrounds.

I turned to Mary and begged, "Come on! Let's take a ride. Please!"

"Just take Adrian with you and be careful," she replied. My friend Adrian didn't know how to swim. It took some convincing, but he conceded.

"Put your life jacket back on! Man, get ready!" I said and took off.

As we were riding back we went under a bridge when suddenly I jerked the engine handle too fast. I lost control of the boat, and out popped the engine. It tumbled into the water and smoke bubbled up as the boat engine sank into the deep lake. I was so scared. I looked over and I could see the worried look on Maribel's face as she yelled from the shore.

"Dive, Beto! You're a good swimmer! Dive and try to find it before Dad finds out! Diiive!"

My friend Adrian was frozen in shock after he almost fell off the boat. He stood trembling and holding on to the edge of the boat for dear life.

Confidence came over me as Maribel screamed "Diiiiiive!" I dove into the water. I searched for that damn engine for a good fifteen minutes. The current was just too fast. I got back on the boat after several tries, gasping for air. It was gone. After I coaxed Adrian to let go of his seat, we paddled back to shore.

When we reached the edge of the lake Maribel was waiting for us with her arms crossed. I pleaded, "You tell Dad. Please, please, Mary."

She sighed and walked away. When we got back to camp she told Dad some story about how someone had forgotten to chain the engine securely to the boat. I was so relieved and mouthed, *"Thank you."*

My parents hired two professional divers and offered them half the worth of the engine if they found it. That was approximately three thousand dollars. Even the divers struggled swimming in that current and ultimately failed to find it. We felt so bad for Dad. We were surprised that he didn't get mad when we returned home. He believed the story Maribel told him.

"I'm just glad you guys are safe," he said, smiled at Maribel and me, and walked back to camp.

EL PASO'S DARKEST DAY

Chapter 3

When we became teenagers, we were required to walk to school, rain or shine, and each of us was taught how to drive a manual transmission. We practiced on an old, stick shift Ford wagon. That old Ford took a beating. At one point one of us would take turns driving it while two of us pushed to "push start" the car, so the battery wouldn't burn out as fast.

As we pushed, we would yell, "Let go! Let off the clutch!" at the driver and off we'd go! That was a really fun way to learn how to drive probably not the safest, but a lot of fun. That wagon was so old and ugly that we parked it three blocks away from school so no one would see us get out of it, on the very rare occasion that our parents let Maribel drive us to school.

When my brothers and I entered Austin High hallways for the first time, you could see African Americans, Caucasians, and Hispanic kids hanging out and giving each other high-fives. Fort Bliss bused in kids that had originated from all over the country. At lunchtime, you could see the African American kids dancing this new dance called break dancing and popping. They had their boom boxes out in the court just doing their moves – poppin' and lockin'. Maribel loved that music, so we ended up hanging out with them a lot.

"Albert, I dare you to dance like them," Maribel would dare me. She always got me with a dare. Before you knew it, I was learning the moves with a few other kids. My sister asked them, "Where did you guys learn to moonwalk like that?"

"In Gary, Indiana," one kid replied, sliding backward down the sidewalk. I didn't expect him to say that, but that's how it was in our school. You never knew where someone could be from.

Maribel made a lot of friends in high school. She hung around with an African American girl named Anaylah. She was smoking hot! She also made friends with Sandra, a white girl, and Virgie, a cute *Chola* girl. The girls had befriended Ferine, who was always a very giddy kind of guy. In hindsight, he may have been gay, but there was no way to know for sure then. Latino men rarely came out with that information. I do know that dude could dance! He taught the girls how to dance disco-like right out of *Saturday Night Fever*.

One morning a white kid we'd never seen before walked off the bus, dressed up all slick. "Hey, dude! Where you from?" I asked.

"New York City."

"*Órale*! Mr. New York City, welcome to our school."

"I'm also a disc jockey. I'll blow you guys out with my jams on prom night! You wait and see!" he replied.

I didn't know what he meant, but, sure enough, on prom night he blew our minds with an awesome light show and great music selection. Kids of all color and races shared one thing there. At that school, we were all Austin High Panthers. We shared two things. We all danced to the music we loved together.

In an industrial area, there was a warehouse that had been converted into a huge dance club for high school kids. It was called *Numbers*. Pretty much all the high school students from around the city went there to dance and compete. When it was time to do a challenge, we would go up on stage and the music would go off! I, Alfredo, and two other guys would be poppin' and lockin' and moonwalking. The Jefferson High kids claimed they got their moves by going to LA clubs. They were good, but we blew them away. The Austin High kids won every dance contest we entered.

One night, when the music stopped, one of the Jefferson High kids approached us and asked, "Where did you dudes learn your moves?"

We replied, "New York City."

"And you, dude. Where you learn to bust out that moonwalk?" he asked, nodding his head at me.

"Gary, Indiana," I replied without hesitation.

***

At the dance contests, my brother Fred had become good friends with a student from Kentucky – Pamela. She was cool. Both she and her brother became family friends. She gave Fred a phone number from one of the military kids. Pamela told him to call her. When he got home, I saw him throw the number in the garbage! I waited for him to go to his room. Then I ran to the trash and picked it out. The paper had the name *Linda* scribbled on it with a phone number. I called that night.

"Hello…Is Linda there?" I asked.

"Who is this?" the girl asked.

"This is Fred… you know…Pamela's friend."

"Oh yeah! Hey!" We spent hours on the phone. She was from Waynesboro Pennsylvania, her mother was a full-blooded

German, and her dad was a serious sergeant in the Army.

The next night we had a blind date at the Northgate Mall. She was gorgeous. She knew right away I wasn't Fred. She teased me about it, but she wasn't mad. I was done - head over heels. At the end of the date, I asked her to be my girlfriend. Linda was my first high school girlfriend.

Maribel and I had some amazing times at that high school.

***

My brothers and I had always walked home with Maribel when we were in middle school. When she became a high school student, Maribel no longer walked with us. Maribel would either walk home with her friends or walk by herself.

There was one day that Maribel walked home alone from school. When she entered the house, she noticed some sounds coming from the living room. She thought it was one of us messing around. She marched into the living room to yell at us, but when she walked in there was a strange, white man sitting at the bar area having a drink. He made eye contact. Then Maribel screamed as loud as she could and sprinted out of the house as fast as she had ever moved! Mrs. Wilson, our neighbor, was watering her lawn with her German shepherd, King, chained up when she heard Maribel screaming.

"Mrs. Wilson! There's a strange man in my house!"

Mrs. Wilson unchained King and led him by the collar to the front door of our house. She let go and commanded, "Sic him, King!" King ran through the front door and knocked the man off the barstool, his glass shattered on the tile as King pinned him to the ground, his paws on his chest. King held him there until the police showed up and cuffed the man.

Later that night we heard a knock on the door. I opened it and there stood an older lady in tears that I didn't recognize.

"Can I talk to your parents?" she asked.

I ran to get my dad. It turned out it was the mother of the man Maribel found in our house.

The lady explained, "That was my son you found in your house. I'm so sorry. My son just got back from the Vietnam War. I think he thought that his grandmother still lived here, so he was waiting for her." She pulled some pictures out of her purse and handed them to my mother. "That's my mother there," she said and pointed to an older woman in a photo who did appear to be in what was then our house. That confirmed the story was true for my parents and they decided to drop all the charges.

From that day on we had to come home earlier so my sister was never alone. This was, of course, only until my father bought Maribel a nice, compact car. Then we never stayed home! That was right on time for her senior year.

Maribel's senior year of high school was the one year we were all in the same high school together. It was awesome! Maribel was confident and comfortable driving around in her car. We mostly went to Billiards to play pool or to McKelligon Canyon - the regular hangout for the local high school kids. My sister had some good-looking friends. Dave and I would ask her to introduce us to them.

"You guys are little punks! Go and find your little girlfriends!" she'd say and blow us off.

On Sundays, we went to Ascarate Lake. Lots of different groups of people would congregate there. As you entered the park, you could see cars cruising around the lake as if it was a boulevard. There was the Z28 Car Club - nothing but new Camaros and Z28's - made up of about forty or so of them. Then you had the Hispanic Bikers that would show off their Harleys. They parked them on the side of the road like they were in a showroom. The Pachucos would parade their beautiful low-riders cruising low and making them hop with hydraulics. They had some awesome cars that they spent a lot of money and time on.

Eventually, some of my friends and I got motorcycles and even formed a group too. We called ourselves "The Boys." Most of us had inexpensive bikes. However, my friend Neto had the very cheapest bike. We constantly had to pull over because his bike broke down. My brother and I usually shared our bikes. Jerry, who is now a high school principal, brought his brother's badass Kawasaki. Ruben's family had way more money and he owned the most expensive bike - the Honda Black Shadow. We named him our leader. He could do a spin-off just like the commercial and he'd do one every time we took off. It was kind of our thing.

Maribel loved spending Sundays at Ascarate chatting with friends, flirting, dancing and just hanging out with people. She just loved to do anything where she was around people.

We were all hanging out at Ascarate and it started to get late - after nightfall, people usually cleared out of Ascarate. We asked Linda and Anaylah, "Hey, you girls want to visit Mexico?"

"I'm not going to no Mexico!" Linda snapped back.

"Come on. Hop on my motorcycle. I'll take you there...Come, Anaylah. Let's go!" It didn't take much coaxing. Anaylah jumped on the back and off we went to a place called La Arboleda.

***

When we arrived at La Arboleda, Linda asked, "What're all those western guys doing wearing cowboy hats?"

"They are "*Cheros*," Maribel answered. This was short for *rancheros*, which are Latino cowboys.

"Mmmm, *Cheros*? They look western to me," Linda replied.

La Arboleda was remarkably similar to Ascarate. The difference was that they showed off their trucks and wore cowboy hats, cowboy boots, huge belt buckles and a great deal of denim. The *Cheros* had big trucks with loud music systems blasting ranchera music, which is like mariachi. One high school friend, Poncho, started coming with us and Maribel. He drove her in his brand-new Ford Bronco. The '*Cheros* showered him with compliments. Whenever someone walked by him they'd stare and say, "nice truck."

The girls eventually decided that they just wanted to hang out in Juarez, Mexico instead so, the very next Saturday, we started going to Juarez Boulevard. We frequented Sarawak, an awesome disco. Tons of high school students from El Paso got together there. You could tell the difference between Mexicans and Americans because the Mexicans went all out. They had their pompadours just right, dressed sharp to the nines. The place was full to the brim, and many El Paso kids were regulars. Maribel loved dancing with her girlfriends, but

EL PASO'S DARKEST DAY

she and Johnny would get down on the floor. They shelled out some serious disco moves. The girls started asking her if he was her boyfriend. She just laughed.

Maribel did marry young, but not to Johnny. I on the other hand eventually married Linda. We even went on to have a family of our own.

Chapter 4

S occer has always been big in the whole region of the Borderland. My father was even the sponsor of a Juarez team. He spent money on sharp uniforms that even my brothers and I wore to the games. The team was in Juarez, so my brothers and I were too young to join, but we were always in the stands cheering them on at the top of our lungs. We were even there during training. My dad never knew his father, so he made sure he was kind to the young guys and tried to be a mentor to them.

Robert was their team captain. He was an athletic guy and became a good family friend. He always showed off in front of my sister. She noticed. Everyone noticed he had a crush on her, from the moment he saw her. Those two often met behind my parent's back and went out on dates! They managed to keep that a secret for quite some time. Eventually, they fell in love, and after another few months, Robert proposed and they decided to get married.

My parents did not like the idea of Mary getting married so young. At the time it was common practice, so my parents' let them. They didn't like it, but they didn't stop them. I don't know if they could've, but they didn't try.

After Maribel and Robert were married, my parents let them create a small apartment in the downstairs of our home. All of us had to move into one room upstairs to accommodate my sister and her husband. My brothers and I decided to play jokes on my brother-in-law. When he was showering, we'd shut off the hot water.

He'd get furious and run out, screaming with his arms waving around, yelling, "Who in the hell is messing with the hot water!"

We'd fall over laughing hysterically while we looked in at everything through the window from outside. All of us grew to like him. He was a cool guy and you could tell Robert was head over heels in love with Mary. It was the beginning of a new chapter in her life.

Since my sister was so young when she got married in turn, she became a very young mother. During her pregnancy, she didn't develop a big belly and kept dancing and having fun. Maribel seemed enthusiastic about her new family. For her age, she acted very mature and was very responsible. I think she was ready to become a mother.

***

When Maribel's beautiful baby girl was born we all instantly fell in love with her - Yvette. All of us pitched in to help raise Yvette. Mary was a fantastic mother.

After a few months, Mary needed some independence and it was getting crowded in the basement. Maribel and Robert decided to move into their own home. Their new home was in Clint, Texas.

Clint was a small rural town at the time. My father was always the cornerstone of our family, so regardless of how far Mary moved he made sure she still spent lots of time at our home. We were a very close-knit family. Many good times were spent with my parents and Maribel's new family.

She did so well that she went on to have one more girl and two boys: Ivonne, Bobby, and Andy. She loved her little family so much. Those were some of her best years just raising her kids. She always had all the family's emotional and physical support. We helped her by babysitting or with whatever she needed for the kids.

On holidays we always got together, especially on Thanksgiving for the Sun Carnival Parade! My father never missed a year...ever! It was a true obsession he had with this parade. He had the utmost respect and admiration for first responders and police, but he was there for the parade! He cheered them on like a little kid.

I'd ask my mother, "Why does Dad get so excited?"

"Because he didn't have a childhood in Mexico," she'd say. I wish I'd asked him more about that, but I never did.

In 1974 we were all watching the parade when a Mexican police officer did a stunt on top of his motorcycle. My dad was the only person who realized that the policeman falling off his motorcycle was not part of the act. He saw the motorcycle flying toward us before anyone else did. Everyone thought it was part of the show.

Dad yelled, "Get out of the way! Here comes that motorcycle by itself!" and he shoved my mother and my brothers and me out of the way. He was just in time as it plunged into the crowd next to us – people jerking to the right and left. A baby flew into the air as the motorbike hit several people.

The baby did survive, but two people died in that accident. My dad continued going to every single parade every year for the rest of his life.

Christmases were a very special time for my father. He gathered us together and we all made tamales. He bought a world encyclopedia around 1970 that he was always dying to use to justify buying it. He would sit at the kitchen table, slowly drinking a beer, and try to prompt us into bringing up certain topics.

Then, no matter what we said, he'd respond, "Okay! Go get an encyclopedia. Let's look it up!" Eventually, we'd all have a big conversation about whatever topic we would lookup. It was a total blast as my father made us have conversations.

Once the sun went down, we'd cruise around the city to look at Christmas lights, but the best ones were right next - door. Before Fred Loya's Christmas Show we had our neighbor - Bob. He went all out with Christmas decorations. Even with our help, it took up to two weeks to decorate his home. It was amazing. My neighbor's house was the hot ticket in the neighborhood! Lines of people formed just to look at his house. We were lucky that we got to see it all the time since we lived next door.

We would always wait until late to open gifts and gather in the living room, just listening to music. We goofed off doing silly moves to the music, but little Bobby took the cake with the best Elvis Presley impersonations ever. Mary would laugh to tears at her son while making all of us laugh.

On just a regular weekend, Mary often spontaneously took her family on road trips. They'd cruise through the desert with the windows down to feel the cool night breeze. They spent nights chitchatting as her kids enjoyed listening to her tell stories of her childhood. She'd make a picnic basket full of sandwiches and snacks. They loved to travel to small towns, like Marfa, where you could see the beautiful shower of stars.

As her kids got older, she started to treat them more like friends. She taught the girls how to line dance to country. Her favorite country singer was Garth Brooks, and we often caught her dancing to Cotton Eye Joe. You could tell Mary loved and cared for all her children so much.

When her kids were a little older and nearing high school, Robert and Mary's relationship started to deteriorate. Mary and Robert began to drift apart. Finally, Mary came over and disclosed that Robert had been unfaithful. She wanted out of her marriage. She had even started looking for another man online to get even. She asked that we all sit

down. We knew where it was headed. She was divorcing Robert. We all tried to talk her out of it and asked if there was anything we could do
to help save her marriage, but it was too late. She left him.

Chapter 5

After Maribel's divorce was official, she decided to meet with a guy she met on the Internet - Leo. They mutually agreed to meet in McAllen, Texas. Leo paid to fly her into town, and they met up in a small restaurant by the beach. They hit it off instantly. For Leo, it was love at first sight. Maribel knew she had found her true love. They had such a connection that Maribel stayed in McAllen longer than planned. We were happy for her, so we didn't mind watching the kids. At some point, they agreed that they would both fly back to introduce Leo to the family.

Mary flew ahead to give us a heads-up. Once she told us we'd be meeting this guy we had to mentally prepare to meet this man that physically swept my sister away to a whole new city and swept away her heart in such a short time. I was skeptical, and my parents were wary since they met on the Internet.

It was Saturday morning when my sister called and implored me, "Please be nice to Leo. It's important to me."

I replied by telling her, "Well, you left your old man for some new one. This better be good." Then off she went to pick up Leo at the airport, while my brothers and I corralled all the family together to be present for his introduction. We were all very cautious and not optimistic. I was pretty much doing the opposite of what Maribel wanted.

When Mary arrived with Leo, we were waiting to see him with curiosity. As he arrived he seemed excited to meet Mary's kids and he looked a little nervous. I presented myself and shook hands with him. He looked young and like a nice guy.

I asked, "Where you from youngster?"

"From the Rio Valley!" he replied with a noticeable accent. I knew right away where he was from. I just wanted to confirm it.

"Yup! I recognize that accent, all right. From the Rio Grande Valley?" I said laughing knowingly. "Welcome to El Paso, Leo!"

My first impression was that he was a likable person. Had my sister just met her true love? I thought…maybe. We have all heard that it's difficult to find your soulmate or someone with whom you have the right chemistry. In my opinion, these two were not a perfect match. How could they be? He was so young, and Maribel didn't know what she was doing. She was just out of a relationship.

As we ate at the table, I could see Maribel's kids just leering at Leo with distrust. After we finished eating, I followed Leo outside and asked him, "Why would you marry an older woman with four kids, Leo? I have to ask."

He said, "I'm in love with Maribel and I'll be a good person with her kids... When you love somebody, you love their presence."

I knew the odds were stacked against him, to marry a woman with older kids. I replied, "Leo, you are a young man. You can still walk away."

He said, "I'm in love with Maribel and age is just a number."

They were married shortly thereafter.

***

Leo and Maribel decided they would both live in the Rio Grande Valley for two years and then live in El Paso for two years alternating indefinitely. Mary took her kids with her and they started a new life. Leo accommodated his new family as best as he could. For such a young man he tried to be a good husband, against all odds. Mary's girls were teenagers, so I can only imagine how difficult it must have been for him.

Leo was a hospitable guy and he took his new family out to the beach on weekends to have a family fun time. He took the boys out to play softball since he was a coach for a Little League team. Bobby began to build a strong bond with him. He was just fourteen years old when they moved and was about to finish his first year of high school.

The girls were older and were very social, so they quickly made new friends, just like their mama. Yvette and Yvonne began to fall in love with the beach. They began dating, so they loved frequenting "the Valley." That's where all the guys were.

***

Once the first two years passed they came to El Paso. It was Leo's turn to enjoy West Texas. Leo made friends fast. He was such a lovable and easygoing guy. Honestly, I never saw him mad or fight with my sister.

My father liked Leo, mainly because he would spark up conversations and was the life of the party. Leo was a bartender as a younger man. He made the best margaritas and mixed

74

drinks I have ever had - to this day. He was an amazing cook and a grill master at heart. He had a karaoke machine that he brought out on weekends and we'd all be singing to different tunes. Leo was a huge mariachi fan, so he'd be blasting that music. My sister loved either that or country.

Leo would serenade Maribel with mariachis for all special occasions. He found any reason to give her flowers, on just ordinary days, and wrote her poetry on Facebook. On Instagram he posted: *Since the day I've met you I knew you were the love of my life.*

I told him, "Leo, I've read your poems on Facebook. Are you copying them from somewhere?" "No, they came from the heart!" he replied.

Maribel's kids were getting older. The girls had been dating a while, which eventually resulted in them getting married and having children of their own. Ultimately, they moved out and Leo, Maribel, and Bobby became a small family of three. Bobby was super close to both and he was with them through bad and good times. Andy lived with his dad and was attending high school.

EL PASO'S DARKEST DAY

EL PASO'S DARKEST DAY

Chapter 6

Mary and Leo now had more time to spend with one another. At this stage of their life, they didn't have the kids around and the two of them became inseparable. They moved back to El Paso where Mary reconnected with old friends, and they both made some new lifelong friends.

Leo and Mary began taking more road trips. They loved to go to San Antonio. On spring breaks, they took their grandkids, and kids to Six Flags, and, their favorite place, Sea World! Leo, being such a fun-loving guy, played the grandpa part so well. He was so crazy about Mary, so I wasn't surprised he was nuts about the kids too. Mary and Leo dressed in matching costumes for each holiday just to see the neighborhood kids' laugh and smile.

I started to see it myself. I really couldn't have been more wrong about them. Leo and Mary were a perfect match. Thank God! I didn't want to be right. I wanted Mary to be happy and I was so happy she was. They were amazing parents to those kids, together as a team. They just fit together in the right way. It was weird. They had a fifteen-year difference between them, but it worked. Maribel looked so young that no one ever noticed their age difference, but it would never have mattered. Those two were made for each other. They were soul mates. When the kids moved out, Leo and Maribel became even closer. It was amazing.

Mary's daughters stayed in the Rio Grande Valley to raise their kids. Yvette often called Mary with the feeling of longing asking, "Hey Mom, can you freeze me some Chico's Tacos and send them to me? I crave them!"

"I'll send you some when I get a chance."

An hour later Ivonne would call. "Hey Mom, can you send me some Chico's Tacos?"

"Okay, hold on...I'll send you some by frozen mail."

Then a couple of hours later Andy would call, "Hey Mom! Can you send me some Chico's Tacos? Mom? Hey Mom? Momma...Dang. Mom hung up on me!"

On weekends Mary and Leo had regular cookouts, especially on sunny days. Leo's cooking was amazing, and he could drink a beer and spark up conversations while doing it without burning a single thing or missing a step. It was a sight to behold full of memories. Leo would always talk about his brothers back home and his beloved mother. He must have been awfully close to his father because he always talked about him the most, and always with pride on his face.

After a few drinks, we all took turns singing different songs on the karaoke machine with the family gathered around. Leo loved singing mariachi. Mary sang freestyle songs from the '80s. One night after karaoke, Mary started telling me she had a dream that she had a huge yard, so her grandkids could run around and enjoy it.

Leo came up behind her and said, "Sure! Of course, we will, babe!" He wrapped his arms around her waist. Leo was a hard-working guy and he'd just gotten a promotion as a call center supervisor with his own team to manage. I knew he meant it!

Leo worked days and went to school at night. During his workday, he talked to many veterans, and he was very good at it. His company handled calls nationally for veterans' medical needs. He showed compassion and treated them with respect, as well as dignity. Bobby always said that Leo told him that he cared about these veterans because they were our true heroes.

With his charming personality, he would greet them on calls, "Hey how are you doing, sir! First, I want to thank you for your service. Now I'm at your service. How can I help you today?"

Mary often stayed up at night helping Leo with term papers. She encouraged him to be the best at what he did. My sister had a big heart, she just had subtle ways of showing it.

Some days she even cooked up hot meals and put them on disposable plates to give to the homeless. She said that she felt they needed someone to show them that love still existed in the world.

In their spare time, Leo and Mary loved to watch movies and stream online videos. One time I walked by their room and I could hear that they were watching videos, so I stuck my head in and said, "Mary, you're going to love this video!"

"Well put it on! What are you waiting for?" she replied. I had been dying to show her this YouTube video that showed how Chicano culture had spread to Japan. The Pachuco culture first started in El Paso, and in Los Angeles, they took it to the extreme. As we watched the video she was cracking up, laughing in disbelief.

She yelled, "Look! There's Virgie!" pointing at a Japanese girl dressed exactly like a Pachuca. Her laugh was infectious, and she had us all doubling over at her reaction.

***

Shortly after Mary moved back to El Paso, my dad passed away. After his passing, my mother became a more devout Christian. It became the rock she needed to make it through my father's death.

My mom then told my brothers, Mary, and I, "You guys need to become involved Christians!"

One Sunday my mother convinced me to go to church with her. The church music group had lost a drummer that day.

My mom told me, "Get on that stage and play the drums, *Mijo*!"

EL PASO'S DARKEST DAY

So, I did because that's my mom. What she says goes.

After a few months of playing with the church band, I fell in love with Christian music. I even decided to become a member of the church. Often, Mom would go on and on explaining to Mary why, and about how, she should become a Christian. For quite some time Mary seemed hesitant about it. I thought Mom should just give up. "She's just going to push her away," I thought.

One afternoon, Mary and Leo both showed up at my mother's house. They approached her, with severity, and said they needed to tell her something.

"What is it?" my mom asked.

"Well, …we have joined a church!"

"Really!" my mother replied with excitement.

"Yes, Mom. I know I am God's child, and He is my King!" said Mary.

"You too Leo?"

"Yes, me too," Leo replied. My mom was so happy. She hugged them both.

***

The following summer Mary's grandkids surprised her and came to visit. She was so ecstatic! They played games, had a cookout, and just hung out enjoying each other's company. Mary began to talk to little Gisselle about God and heaven. She explained to Gisselle about how one day we are all going to pass on and when we do, we will eventually meet in heaven. After that talk, they continued with their day filled with laughter and joy. Mary had a ton of fun with her grandkids. She watched movies with them, played games, and ran around outside. Her grandkids told me Mary was extremely happy just being with them in anything they did, even if it was for just one day.

After the grandkids headed out on Saturday morning, Mary and Leo decided to go camping at Ruidoso with Bobby. It was always an adventure just going to Ruidoso. They jammed out in the car and sang along to their favorite songs.

When they'd reach Ruidoso, Mary would say, "We are in God's country!" and she'd stretch her arms out toward the sky. Then she'd clap her hands together and say, "Okay, let's go guys. Set up camp."

Once the sun went down, Mary and Leo would sit on the ground looking up at the stars, while they talked about their plans to look for a new home once they got back. They spent the precious moments they had on that weekend, showing their love for one another. They played cards with Bobby, cracked jokes, and laughed. Those three had an unbreakable bond.

Leo told Mary, "Let's come back next weekend. I love it out here."

Mary said, "Maybe, but you know we have things to do next weekend. We have errands."

***

That Sunday evening, as the three of them drove back home, out of the blue while they were talking in the car, Bobby said, "Hey Leo. I just wanted to let you know we're best friends and we will always be. But I also wanted to say you are like a dad to me."

Leo said, "Oh come on Bobby! You know that I already adopted you a long time ago." They both burst out laughing with the biggest smiles on their faces. He was always a dad to him.

***

The following Monday started as a regular weekday. Both Leo and Bobby had gone off to work and Mary was preparing food for them. She tended to her garden, which was filled with beautiful *Bugambilias*.

The following Saturday morning, Mary decided to go out to take her dog, Fiji, to the groomers, and buy some items to throw a cookout.

Before she left, she went to Bobby and asked, "Hey lazy bones, do you want to come with me?"

Bobby replied, "I think I'll pass. I had a long night. I'm going to stay in for today."

Mary smiled. "Okay. See you later. Love you - bye!" she said and off she went to Walmart.

EL PASO'S DARKEST DAY

Chapter 7

t was a bright, sunny day on Saturday, August 3, 2019. I had just dropped off a customer at the airport. I did the occasional ride-hailing as a side job to bring in some extra money. I had two teenagers to take care of, so money rapidly disappeared. Once I finished dropping my passenger off, I went home to get in touch with my kids and ask if they wanted me to make them lunch.

My daughter jumped up in excitement, "Can you make Chinese food?"

I could never say no to her, so I agreed and headed out to the grocery for ingredients.

The recipe took a while to cook, so I was quick to get the items and drove straight back.

When I arrived at the house, my kids were in the living room glued to their phones and making comments to each other without eye contact. Just another day, so I thought nothing of it.

"A typical day with kids in the technology era," I mumbled to myself and snickered as I walked to the kitchen to set my supplies on the counter. I put my phone down next to the bags when suddenly it buzzed in a weird pattern. I assumed it was an amber-alert or a weather notification, but when I looked at the screen, it said: Active Shooter Alert.

Staring at my phone I was in complete shock. My kids' voices from the other room snapped me out of the haze. I rushed to the TV and switched the channel to the news. I couldn't believe what I was seeing. I saw images of a horror that was unfolding. There was a chaotic situation at the Cielo Vista Walmart. At the time, the media didn't have much information. There was a huge police presence and reporters were saying that there was one, or maybe two, armed men involved in an active shooting situation. The news just kept saying that there could be multiple shooters.

Moments after turning on the news, my son said, "Dad! You won't believe this, but photos are circulating on social media of a shooter entering a store with an assault rifle!"

"How can you be sure that is real?" I replied. My kids handed me their phones. "There are photos of people lying on the ground dead!" I shouted after I'd scrolled through a few of the videos and photos my kids showed me. People were being tragically shot down and lay lifeless on the floor. At first, I just froze in disbelief again. El Paso had been a relatively safe city for so long. I questioned that this was real. "No WAY! This can't happen. Why here in El Paso?" I said to myself in a soft voice. I just couldn't imagine this could be happening in El Paso, but the sheer number of videos, photos, and news coverage forced me to accept this as reality.

Once I came to accept that what I had seen was happening, I knew this had to be a terrorist attack. We were so close to the United States border. I continued to watch the news with my kids. We saw footage of people being carried out on shopping carts bleeding. I couldn't get clear-cut confirmed information about what was truly going on; between the news reporting, the videos posted on the Internet, and the police not saying much. Suddenly I realized that this was my cousin Jaime's work shift.

I grabbed my phone and clicked his image. He worked a regular shift at the Sears in Cielo Vista Mall. As soon as Jaime picked up I was relieved to hear his voice and yelled, "Jaime! What the hell is going on over there? It's all over the news that there's a shooter!"

My cousin replied shouting over sirens and other people's voices, "I don't know! We just suddenly heard gunshots from far away! They're evacuating the mall now! There are police everywhere!" I could barely make him out with all the background noise. "People are being brought out with their hands up by

SWAT teams! And there are cops everywhere! I'm going to have to go! I have to get people out of here! I'll talk to you later. We have to lock the store!"

My wife and I were in shock as we both watched the news unfold. I moved my fingers as fast as I could over my phone to contact my family and friends about how they should stay away from the Cielo Vista area. While we kept watching the situation unfold, helpless, I was thankful to have my children and my wife in the safety of our living room. An El Paso police spokesman came on the news and said they believed it was a terrorist gang-related shooting. It was a terrible and heartbreaking sight. You could see people coming out of the stores and mall entrances with their arms raised, and policemen escorting people who were injured. People were being pushed on carts - men, women, teens, and children crying. They all looked so defeated and horrified.

I kept asking myself, "Who would be responsible for this? Could it be a terrorist cell from a foreign country?" I prayed the police would capture whoever was responsible. I prayed they would have some justice, and at the same time, I was so relieved that my kids were with me, safe. They shopped at the Cielo Vista Mall often, and that day they stayed home with me instead. I thank God with all of my being for that.

It was maybe only a few more hours before the El Paso police made a statement on the news that an arrest had been made, and in fact, it was a terrorist attack on our community. We sat anxiously to see who was responsible for this brutal attack that shook our beloved city to its core. The police went on to state that they had the situation under control and that they believed the events to have been entirely executed by a lone gunman. We waited impatiently as the police department finally released a photo. A twenty-one-year-old Caucasian male from Allen, Texas had been detained and charged after he confessed to police. They put his picture on television and I couldn't believe what I was seeing. This very evil young man had been the person who caused this devastation and loss. He wasn't much older than my children.

I was surprised at how relieved I felt that an arrest had been made. I grabbed my kids and hugged them both. I looked in their faces and told them, "I thank God every second that you are here with me."

An American had carried out a vicious attack on our community. A person from our state had come to kill innocent human beings. The police went on to announce the number of people who had been shot and that the victims had been taken to two different hospitals that were both only minutes from the site. The medical staff was alerted, and all available doctors had been rushed to both hospitals. I knew there was a level one trauma unit at University Medical Center by the Walmart and that Vista Del Sol Medical Center was nearby as well, so I knew those must've been the two hospitals they were referring to. I drove by them all the time. The news said approximately twenty were declared dead at the scene and many were injured. They gave no indication about which victims went where. And there was no word about the deceased or their whereabouts.

I looked at the wall clock and saw it was around three-thirty p.m. That's when I realized we hadn't heard from Mary. She should've called one of us by now.

I thought, "She might have been busy with something or out of town, so I shouldn't be worried. She could be okay."

Shortly thereafter, my phone rang. It was my mother. "Albert! The dog groomer called, and she said Mary hasn't picked up Fiji from the groomers. The dog groomer said it wasn't like your sister not to pick up the dog so late and that Fiji's getting anxious... I'm worried!" Her voice cracked with the same concerns I then started to have. I needed to find Maribel.

"I'll call Bobby to check up on her," I replied and hung up to call Bobby.

"Bobby," I said when he answered and asked, "Have you heard from your mom? The groomers just called and said Fiji didn't get picked up yet." I tried so hard to restrain myself, to control the tone in my voice. I didn't want Bobby to panic.

I could tell Bobby had just woken up as soon as he started talking, "I'll call them. Let me check…they could be at the casino." Bobby paused a long time and then went on to say, "I could track her phone to see where she's at."

My heart raced while I waited for Bobby to call back.

When the phone finally rang, I answered, and Bobby was hysterical. "I've traced my mom's phone!"

"Where is it?"

"It's at the Walmart!" he said in a frenzy. "Not only is it at the Walmart it's inside the store!" Bobby screamed.

"Okay. I'll come to get you. We're going to look for her."

At that time, all the family had begun to get in touch with one another. We arranged to get together to form a search team to find Maribel.

We began making phone calls and driving around nonstop until someone could tell us where to find Mary. Her kids searched all hospitals in the city. We were trying to go to Walmart, but we were turned away. The news wouldn't give us any information. We called Leo to see if he knew where Mary could be, but there was no answer.

Chapter 8

We searched for hours into the night, with no success. We all decided to head out to the reunification center, which was in an elementary school. The El Paso Independent School District (ISD) Police were out in full force-carrying AR-15 semi-automatic assault rifles. As we entered the elementary school you could see FBI agents, US marshals, state police and the local El Paso Police, as well as chaplains, and many other first responders speed- walking about the building.

When we met up with Maribel's other kids, they were sitting with a bunch of other families who were searching for people as well. You could see the worry and tension in their faces. Many were motionless and in shock. I walked into another room and saw the coroner's office staff and the chaplains and I immediately thought the worst. My heart started to race. We were all hoping and praying that it wouldn't be one of us that got the bad news. We didn't want my mother to be present because she is an older woman and the scene was so stressful. My mother would call us to get updates all night worried and terrified.

She was shaking and just kept asking, "Where is Mary? ... How can you guys not find her? ... She can't be lost. I know it. Where is she?"

It wasn't long before our mayor, Dee Margo, and the Texas governor, Greg Abbott, were there to address our group. Dee Margo looked stunned by all that had happened. You could see the concern all over his face as he spoke, "I can't explain why someone would commit such a terrible and heinous crime against our community. When situations are unexplainable and horrific, I look to my Bible to try and find answers."

The Governor then spoke. "This tragedy will change lives. I made it through a serious accident a while ago that left me in a wheelchair. We should ready ourselves and pray."

They both might have said more but at the moment that was all I heard. Half of my mind was present, and half was consumed with dread.

I noticed some Juarez families sitting to my left, with a man that was in tears asking if his wife was dead. He and his son had seen his wife shot inside the store near the bank.

"Why won't they tell us who was killed? I need to know!" the man shouted.

I saw Mary's kids still seemed to have hope. I didn't want to talk to them. I didn't want to tell them the worst-case scenario that kept whirling through my mind.

The police gave periodic briefings to us, saying that they could not give out any information and that it would take a while for families to get the answers they sought. Everyone had to be patient. It was hard when it's about whether someone you love is dead or alive or wounded.

Suddenly an older African American man yelled out, "Was there a black man shot?"

I instantly mumbled to myself, "This evildoer shot people of all races." I knew he didn't care what race they were. He was just a killer. Then I saw a Caucasian family as well, which confirmed for me that this terrorist must have shot without regard to any ethnicity.

The night dragged on, and the police weren't saying anything except that they wanted us to wait there until morning. I made an approximate count of the families there and it was close to twenty.

I told the police, "I made a count of the families and there are only twenty. Can you just tell us who was killed?"

A man from Juarez announced to everyone, "Raise your hands to make a count of the families that are present!"

Someone from each family raised their hand, and sure enough, I was right. At that point, people started to break down crying.

Mary's kids decided to stay and wait through the night for any information. I went home to call other family members of both Leo and Maribel.

I told everyone, "Be ready...it doesn't look like Mary or Leo survived the attack." I wished they did, but I had a horrible feeling in my gut.

That night I tried to get a few hours of sleep. I must have slept for just that amount when I was woken up by a dream early that morning as the sun rose. My father appeared to me in my dream after I saw a bright light.

In a calm, soothing voice he said, "Don't look for Maribel anymore. She is with me now." I woke my wife and told her about the dream. I asked her to come with me to the reunification building.

As we drove back, I went with a heavy heart. I could feel she was gone, but if they officially gave us the news that would make it final. There would be nothing I could do to get her back. There would be nothing I could do to change that if they told us Mary or Leo was gone. I had to know, but I didn't want to.

When my wife and I approached the building, the same families were there that we had seen before. They were grieving. I saw Mary's kids with distraught faces, crying hysterically. I knew. My worst thoughts had come to fruition. Mary and Leo had been shot and killed.

The police had finally explained some of the details of the events during the day prior to shooting. Mary's kids couldn't talk, but I asked some of the family members who were more composed about what was said. A man from Juarez reiterated all the information the police gave them.

Our city had experienced, what they described as, the worst domestic terrorist

EL PASO'S DARKEST DAY

attack against Latinos in American history. According to different sources, the shooter drove from his home in Allen, Texas, which was over a nine-hour drive, to kill as many Hispanics and Mexicans as possible. When he arrived in El Paso, he stayed at a hotel near the Walmart and on August 3, he was staking out the Cielo Vista Mall area, looking for an opportunity to attack with the highest number of victims in the shortest time.

He must have found out or someone must have told him to go to that Walmart where Mexicans shop. It worked. He found his target; however, it didn't stop there. The people that shop at the Cielo Vista Walmart are synonymous with what makes up El Paso - people of all races. He killed white and black people along with the Hispanics. He killed children, mothers, fathers, and grandparents indiscriminately. His intention may have been to murder Mexicans, but he ended up committing a blind and ignorant slaughtering of innocent lives. Perhaps because he never really knew what he was looking for. He never really understood how similar we all are.

That man drove up to the store armed with an AK-47 rifle and as much ammunition as he could carry. I guess he was hungry because he went into Walmart and bought some food first. Some people reported seeing the man walk out with hatred and evil eyes. He went to his car, grabbed his assault rifle, and immediately got out of the car with protective eyeglasses and ear protectors on. He started opening fire from beside his car. He shot a couple of people in the parking lot and more in the front of the store as he walked in. He entered the store with his shooting gear exposed. The store manager noticed him and saw a man collapsed in the parking lot, lying motionless. The well-trained manager, on instinct, called code brown -Walmart's code for a mass shooting.

The manager yelled for people to run, over and over, in English and Spanish, *"Corran! People and employees run, for your lives!"*

The shooter proceeded toward the McDonald's that was located inside the Walmart. A woman saw him and threw her mother under a table. The elderly woman hid there with her legs twisted. Sylvia's phone was recording unintentionally, which went viral of a man being shot. The shots were loud, like a train clicking on the rails. The shooter went down aisles, shooting people with no regard for human life, no regard for women or children. He just shot and shot. Some described the look on his face as pure evil as he walked through the store shooting as many people as he could find.

When he was done, the shooter walked back to his car. A witness reported seeing the man get into his car and he appeared to have jammed his weapon. The area was immediately surrounded by the most massive police presence in El Paso history. The suspect then drove as fast as he could through the parking lot, attempting to dart through each exit. When he was unable to flee the confines of the parking lot, the El Paso police were able to surround him. The suspect raised his hands and was arrested. The final victim count was twenty-six people injured and twenty-two people killed.

Two things were done right that day: the speed at which the grounds of the Walmart were surrounded by the police, and the two closest hospitals were prepared for the incoming casualties. People's lives were saved that day because of their rapid call to action.

After a while of being detained by law enforcement, the shooter confessed to the El Paso Police Department that he was there to kill as many Mexicans as he could. I was wrong about it all. I'd so confidently concluded that he was just a killer, but he wasn't just shooting people of any race. He didn't just lack the value of human life. He was trying to shoot only Latinos. He was stupid and shot all kinds of people, but he was targeting the Latino community specifically. The shooter's final post on a hate website reflected the pungency of hatred: "Keep up the good fight," (Evans 2019).

EL PASO'S DARKEST DAY

Chapter 9

The weeks following the darkest day in the history of El Paso further revealed the depth of the atrocities committed, as well as the triumph over evil. As names and pictures began to circulate through the media you could see the sheer number of victims impacted. The community began to unite to overcome this evil. The biggest demonstration was how people lined up in huge numbers to donate blood to help the wounded, and how the donations poured into local charities. El Paso became stronger!

Maribel's children had gone through a crisis and were understandably distraught. My brothers and I took them under our wings for a while. They couldn't come to terms with not having a reason for why this would happen to them.

"Why us? Why!" Mary's kids kept asking.

I could only tell them, "I think we got caught up in a deadly cancer that has plagued our country. We need to stay strong and in control. We need to stay focused and we need to prepare for funeral arrangements."

***

The Tuesday after the attack I received a call and I answered, "Hello?"

A voice replied, "*Hola! Hermano* Albert! How are you and your family doing?"

"Who is this?"

118

"This is Angel, from Operation Hope. My condolences. I have good news *Hermano*! Tell your family not to worry about funeral expenses! Everything will be covered!"

"Thank you! Thank you so very much!" I replied and asked, "Is this covering only Maribel's funeral, or will Leo also be covered?"

"Well, local funeral directors have told us that they will cover everyone at whatever the cost, and to tell all families not to worry." Later I was able to meet Angel. He was this big Hispanic man that dressed like a *Cubano*. A very kind and enthusiastic guy!

The FBI remained all over town not only doing investigations but also helping families. They assigned agents to handle families' concerns and questions. They provided transportation to family members that were coming from out of town for funerals. Sadly, they had experience dealing with these mass shootings and they were prepared on the protocol for helping communities who had been victimized such as ours.

Media had come from all over the world to the Walmart site to try to obtain interviews with people. Understandably, this was the first mass shooting of its kind in the U.S. (targeting Latinos). Why someone would commit such a horrible act of violence on innocent people was difficult to grasp in the general public's mind. Maribel's children wanted to stay anonymous, and they didn't want to talk to any of the media. I didn't visit the Walmart site until weeks later. It was full of people paying respects for the victims, but I couldn't.

My wife and I were at my mother's house when our neighbor, Mrs. Uribe, came to visit. She asked if one of us could give an interview with her niece from KFOX 14 Houston.

I asked, "Who's she?"

"It's Chrisdyann!" she replied and showed us a photo on her phone. We recognized her instantly from pictures at Ms. Uribe's. We grew up with Jerry Uribe, her dad and, of course, agreed to the interview.

She came over the next day and asked us a variety of questions about the recent events as she held back tears.

"This hit too close to home," she said as she nodded her head while my mother and I took turns answering. Her face was solemn the whole visit and we appreciated that she could relate to what we had been through - having grown up here in El Paso. Other reporters were just gathering information, but she knew our community as a member.

I told Chrisdyann about how the shooter had left behind a ridiculous, unfounded, and ignorant rant against Hispanics. The killer claimed that Hispanics were invaders in

America. When I heard that, so much frustration rose inside me. I knew that the Mexican nationals that were shot were here in El Paso simply shopping, wasting their hard-earned money. These Mexicans were law-abiding citizens who had legal documentation to cross over to El Paso. They had no intention to stay in the United States. They had their homes and families in Mexico. They were not invaders or a danger to our country. They were just shopping in support of our local economy. The Texas Borderland, which is a binational metropolitan area of a few million people, depends on both Mexican and American nationals economically.

Further, I explained how I knew that my grandfather, from Mexico, was a white man with Spanish blood and my grandmother was an indigenous native from Mexico. Our ancestors were of the same European descent that the lunatic sought to preserve. Our ancestry goes way back. We have been here for a long time. We resided in this area before his existence. He didn't know his victims and he didn't accomplish anything he set out for. He didn't know American history at all! He should have opened up a book and learned something about his own country's past before unloading a weapon in a public place, aimed at families and infants that he surmised were illegally in the U.S. This terrorist had gotten himself in a very dire situation for a very ignorant reason.

That evening the news began publicly releasing all the names of the victims that had passed away. One by one victims appeared on the news.

A family that really stood out to us as more tragic than the rest was the Anchondo family.

They were a young couple that died protecting their two-month-old son from the gunman.

None of it made any sense. *How?... How can this happen? How? Who would ever think that our city would go through such a horrible ordeal due to such a senseless act of violence?*

These are the questions that circulated through my mind. These are the questions my neighbors and loved ones kept asking each other. My family and I sat gathered in the living room, watching what seemed like unending tragedy and loss. We prayed for the Anchondos, their family, and their baby that survived now without a mother or father.

I recognized some of the families that were mentioned from that dreadful day at the reunification center. The Johnsons - their family member died shielding his family. That man that was looking for a black-man was related to or was a friend of, Chris Grant - a survivor that was shot twice but recovered. Mrs. Englisbee's daughter had been seen frantically looking for her mother. Ultimately her mother was located among the dead. So many victims were affected by this terrorist act: twenty-two dead and twenty-six injured.

I wish I didn't, but I knew what those families were going through as they announced the deaths of Maribel and Leo. I could just imagine the twenty other families that were going through the same thing on both sides of our border. We all eventually had to go through the same painful process, of burying our dead.

***

The day came for us to see Leo for the last time. As we walked into the viewing room, it was packed to the brim with people. There were lots of reporters from different stations lining the walls. Leo was a well-liked man in our community and his hometown of McAllen, Texas. This is where it all culminated for me how heinous this shooting was. I saw my brother-in-law there, lying in a coffin; a beautiful, vibrant person now lay lifeless. That was so hard for me and my family to see his gentle, kind face affectless forever - all due to a senseless act of extreme violence.

Beto O'Rourke made an appearance to mourn his fellow El Pasoans. I'd heard he was on a presidential campaign, but according to the news, he'd halted it to be there for his community. I was surprised to see him there with us at the funeral, toe to toe with my family and friends. When we talked to him he listened patiently, and I found some comfort in having a member of our government assure us that the nation was behind us. I believed him too.

The following day, our congresswoman, Veronica Escobar, contacted us to let us know that there would be an American flag given to Leo at the funeral home and that flags had been flown at half-staff at the White House and all government buildings, per President Trump's order, for all the lives lost at the El Paso shooting.

Angel called shortly thereafter, to inform us that he had arranged to have Leo flown back to his hometown. This was so he could be laid to rest close to his family. My brother, his stepson, and I rushed to drive over there to pay our last respects one more time. I had asked my family members to try to be respectful to the media while I was gone. The attention, when everyone just wanted to grieve, was frustrating, but I knew this was not a time for division. It was a time for unity, and I didn't want that terrorist to get any satisfaction from this.

I was really worried about Bobby with all the reporters that kept coming to interview us. Especially when one reporter asked me, in front of him, "Why an American flag to Leo?"

I told him, "Because he was an American and a proud Texan."

Bobby was sitting with his head bowed. A reporter turned to him for a comment and asked, "How are you related to Leo?"

To my amazement, Bobby looked her right in the eyes and said, "He was my stepdad. And cherish your loved ones, because you never know when they can be taken away from you." His eyes watered, but he was locked onto her gaze. She became flustered and ended the interview.

***

Later that week we held the viewing for my sister.

Many of our family members from all different states came to her funeral. They were in shock that this terrorist act happened in our community. They felt directly affected by it, being mostly Latino Americans. Beto O'Rourke, our mayor - Dee Margo, and the mayor's wife were in attendance. Our mayor from the start was incredibly supportive, and I was pleasantly surprised he was so on top of things. He gave us his card and tried to offer words of solace to me and my family by assuring us that he was there for us, as well as all the rest of the victims, should we ever need anything.

As we left the church I could, with all sincerity, say that my sister had the most beautiful funeral I had ever been to. The One for Life Christian Church had a gorgeous ceremony. The pastor gave an inspiring speech. As the mass ended, and the pallbearers loaded Maribel into the hearse, six sheriffs on motorcycles escorted her to the cemetery to join our father where he lay. It is a beautiful final resting place for her.

I'm not a preacher by any means, but I have tried to study the Holy Bible in detail. I told my children and family that I am convinced that we must all be fallen angels reincarnated into this world as humans. Adam and Eve were cast out of heaven to come and make things right with God again.

Whatever happened to the one-third of the other angels that were cast out of heaven? Most people think that we have a purpose in this life. I think it's to make things right with Almighty God. Well, Maribel and Leo have done just that. They have fulfilled their loyalty to God, and they are living in heaven with their King.

Chapter 10

The other families of the victims were finishing burying their loved ones. Once the last funeral was complete, that's when the El Paso Strong movement began gaining momentum. The families and the community were done with the logistics. El Paso wanted to direct their grief toward action. People wanted to do something! The aim of the movement was for the city of El Paso to move forward. And we all were more than ready.

We focused on our heritage. I took upper-division classes in Chicano Studies at the University of Texas at El Paso (UTEP). I learned about how our forefathers were of Spanish descent. When I say Spanish, I'm referring to European Spaniards. The Spanish settlers had ruled El Paso for over two hundred and twenty years before the United States had formed. Spanish was the first European language spoken in North America. The Spanish conquistadors had a caste system where the full-blooded Spanish were plantation owners. That's why you see a great deal of white Hispanics today - because of the Spaniards' presence.

When the Spanish settlers began to have children with the indigenous people, their children were called Mestizos. Mestizos are descendants of white European and Native Americans. Most Latino residents of El Paso are Mestizos and they have been here for a very long time. Our native ancestors occupied the area far before the European arrival. The classification of US Hispanics had been distorted throughout time.

I started to become curious about my history. As I dug into my family's ancestry, I discovered that most Hispanics are Mestizos. I recalled memories of being scared when my *Abuela* brought my siblings and me to see "Indians" dancing with scary masks when we were children. I now realize we were watching a Mexican Native American dance. It doesn't make me have any fewer nightmares about it, but it's nice to know our family dates back that far in North American history. I was even happier to have proof that at the end of the day we are all Americans.

I was at UTEP doing research when I received a call from Holly at KFOX requesting an interview with me regarding the El Paso Strong movement. I agreed to it. I was eager to talk about the progress we'd made, and for the terrorist to see that he hadn't beaten us.

During the interview, I told Holly, "Here in El Paso we have the cream of the crop when it comes to different races. We have a good mix of people in this city and they have always gotten along well. There was an instance where I was waiting in line at a supermarket, and I saw a Latina woman short on money to buy her groceries. A black man told the woman, 'Don't worry,' and took out his debit card to pay for all her groceries. The man left smiling in satisfaction and the lady was left with her mouth hanging open in disbelief. That woman couldn't believe the act of kindness, but that's how a lot of people are around here."

I told Holly about how we have many military soldiers in the community who had offered their lives to protect this country. I have seen military sergeants from Fort Bliss that had been through gruesome battles in various countries around the world, and they were still able to show kindness. The soldiers I'd pass when shopping at the grocery store, or in the mall, were always polite. Thousands of young soldiers from around the country of all races, in our community, that were still nothing but courteous.

They address you, "Yes sir… No sir!" The Army has done something substantial concerning race relations. It's probably that in the US Army there's no time for nonsense. Everyone must get along because your life may depend on the person next to you, regardless of his or her race. The US soldiers have one flag that they all fight for.

The El Paso area is no stranger to helping troops mend after conflict. The El Paso Star has shined bright for our soldiers while they were away in combat. When the Iraq War broke out, the first prisoners of war were Fort Bliss soldiers - women and men. Our city was on edge as we saw troops from our

city held captive. We posted yellow ribbons on many trees to show solidarity until their release.

Since my family's original move to El Paso, I've seen a cultural boom. El Paso's citizens now come from all over the world due to its growth. I've met people who now reside in El Paso who came from India, Hawaii, the Middle East, and as far as the Pacific Islands. I think what attracts people is the friendliness, the affordable housing, the mild winters, and that it's a developed area that is still not overly

EL PASO'S DARKEST DAY

crowded. El Paso has become a city of true diversity.

I told Holly, "You know…some people are saying jealousy and hate was a contributing factor to his actions…because the shooter must have had some knowledge of our city's makeup besides just thinking there are Hispanics."

"Maybe."

"Well…some local politicians are saying that he attacked the core of who we are as a community. El Paso has been a safe city for such a long time. The terrorist just found an opportunity to attack our city completely off-guard. This city wasn't prepared to have such a horrific incident occur here, but we came together strongly!"

***

The city of El Paso went on to unite the victims and the families that were impacted through different public events. One such event was attendance at a game with our minor league baseball team, the Chihuahuas. They gave my family and me entrance to VIP! This was the first event where we got the chance to talk to other victims since the attack. We had the opportunity to share stories with people who'd gone through the same pain. Most of the families that had any losses were there. We talked and offered condolences.

I started talking to a young man and when we formally introduced ourselves, I learned he was Andre Anchondo's younger brother. I introduced him to my family. We all told him we were sorry for his loss and that our hearts were with his family.

He said, "You know…my brother practiced martial arts and was athletic. I can't be sure, but a witness said that my brother might have been trying to wrestle the assault rifle from the shooter."

"A true hero. Hey man, how's the baby doing?" I asked.

"He's okay…"

"So, what else is new? Are you okay?"

"…Oh! We met the First Lady of the United States! She carried the baby and offered condolences of course," he replied. "She seems like a very nice woman and she is beautiful indeed," he added.

There were a few other celebrities at the event as well. Edward James Olmos was going around to visit with the families. When he approached ours, I said, "*Órale*! Miami Vice!"

My daughter rolled her eyes and said, "Dad! You didn't just say that!"

"What? We used to love to watch this guy on Miami Vice!"

Olmos just laughed. He is such a nice guy. He told us how he was there to show support. Everybody took pictures with him. It was exciting in a good way!

Then George Lopez walked in. He'd been rumored to have been at local hospitals visiting patients. "*Órale*! George Lopez!" He was also there to support the families and, of course, he held back his jokes. Nice to see that popular comedian there that day.

"Dad! Please! You need to stop saying *Órale*. You're embarrassing me. It's George Dad! Come on!" my daughter yelled. I loved when she turned red like that. It was so funny.

Several speakers were featured, including Governor Abbott, the mayor of Juarez, and Governor Corral of Chihuahua. When Governor Corral spoke, he demanded a thorough investigation of the Walmart shooting. The Mexican government had been vocal about wanting the U.S. to extradite the suspect to Mexico to face charges. Now there he would have experienced instant justice.

After the politicians were done with their speeches, the El Paso Police Department officers were given recognition for capturing the shooter. The crowd applauded with a standing ovation. I just wish they'd have acknowledged some of the other heroes from that dreadful day.

The memorial ended with twenty-two *candelas* lit in remembrance of the deaths, and a spectacular fireworks display. The county jail where the suspect was being held was so close to the stadium.

I imagined the shooter and said to myself, "I hope you can hear these fireworks. You messed with the wrong city and you will hear from us again." I wished he could hear me. I still felt so much anger. I knew the healing process wasn't going to be a fast one. It was going to take time. I felt moments of rage throughout the day. I just accepted it and went on with my responsibilities. Focusing on what was in front of me.

As a young man I worked in Texas corrections and for a while, I worked in corrections in New Mexico as well. I even worked with death row inmates before. I knew this, and I could tell all the victims this: that evildoer is in hell on earth. I know he's under constant lock and key and I'm positive he detests his new environment. I take solace in that. This man crossed a line into a place that no man wants to be in, and one that you can never come back from. There will come a point when he will ask for death to come, and it won't. This creature doesn't believe in

Almighty God. He decided to run towards evil. He should tremble at his death for Almighty God detests evildoers and his judgment will be swift. For not only is he an enemy of the United States of America, but he is an enemy to all that is good. There is no place for him in what we all know as heaven, but there is a ripe seat in hell waiting for him. But we all know that. We know the attacker is human garbage, we know he's going to receive punishment and suffer the rest of his life and beyond. What else is there? What do we do now? Where do we find the light?

On that dark day, many stepped up. Some heroes gave their lives so that others may live. Let's talk about the heroes and their heroic deeds. Some people waited until the perfect opportunity to help and some jumped in to protect their fellow man. Many eyewitness accounts of such actions were told and should be remembered for generations to come.

Andre Anchondo, twenty-three and Jordan Anchondo, twenty-four, died shielding their two-month-old baby. It was a very normal sunny day when they went shopping at Walmart. They must have made a split-second decision when they were surprised and ambushed. Andre Anchondo used himself as a human shield to protect his wife, Jordan, who covered her two-month-old infant with her body to keep him safe. The young couple sacrificed themselves so their son could live, and he did.

Dave Johnson was a sixty-three-year-old Army veteran, NASCAR fan, and golf enthusiast. He died after ordering his wife and nine-year-old granddaughter to get down. He fell on his family after being shot to give them cover. He must have made the quick decision to save his family knowing he would not make it - a courageous act of love. His wife and granddaughter lived.

Jorge Calvillo Garcia, a sixty-one-year-old accountant, shielded his granddaughter and as much as he could of her soccer team from bullets. He was also a hero. A man that cared so much for his granddaughter that he used his body to save not only her but her fellow teammates.

Juan De Dios Velázquez, a seventy-seven-year-old man who moved from Mexico with his wife, Nicolasa, to El Paso after obtaining U.S. citizenship as retirees. He and his wife were in Walmart and the shooter approached Mr. Velázquez who moved in front of his wife. He was shot in the back and ultimately passed away. His wife was shot in the abdomen, but she survived.

Mario De Alba, a forty-five-year-old Mexican national, was shopping with his nine-year-old daughter and his wife. He was shot in the back while protecting his family. He and his family survived. Mario is still in critical condition in his hometown of Chihuahua, Mexico.

Guillermo "Memo" Garcia recently died after a being in the hospital for nine months. He and wife Jessica were both shot while protecting their children. He was called " Tank" cause he was a big guy with a big heart.

Then you had Lazaro Ponce who also survived the attack. He was a homeless transient living in a camp nearby Walmart at the time of the shooting. He saw the gunman shooting people and he hid until he had the opportunity to help the wounded. When he thought it was safe, he ran toward a crying baby and picked him up from under his mother, who did not survive and ran him out to first responders. He then re-entered the Walmart to get towels to wrap around victims' gunshot wounds. He was another hero that helped save lives.

We don't know how Maribel or Leo went down. Only the police know exactly what happened to them. We do know Mary had a receipt from Walmart and her body was found on the ground near the front of the store. In a video from a woman that survived, I could see someone that looks like my sister looking at the camera with fear in her eyes after a man was shot. First responders say they saw a woman down on the ground with a man on top of her that may have been Mary and Leo. When their bodies were recovered, Leo had been shot in the back and my sister in her torso. Those wounds are consistent with others who had attempted to protect their loved ones by shielding them with their bodies. If I was guessing, based on all I know about them, Leo tried to save Maribel. That's my intuition. What we know for certain is that they left this world together - Maribel Hernandez at the age of fifty-six and Leo Campos at forty-one-years of age. I know that they are loved and missed and survived by four amazing children.

***

The Grand Candela was unveiled at the site of El Paso's darkest day on Saturday, November 23, 2019. The night before, a private lighting was held with all the families of the victims and all survivors. It looks like a giant golden candle. The exact height of the memorial is thirty-feet tall and it's made up of twenty-two aluminum arcs that illuminate and are grouped together. The arcs shine light up into the sky. The Grand Candela forever remembers the lives lost, as well as the community unification in El Paso. Our city was put through a test and it made us come together, as well as strengthened us as individuals.

At the end of the day we know where the twenty-two victims are. We can't ever let hate win or take over our hearts. This event doesn't define us as to who we are as a binational community. Let our angels shine and let us remember them as a symbol of what we are in El Paso. We are friendly, we are cheerful, and we are resilient to overcome evil. We care about our people, as we have demonstrated again and again. The community healing had begun.

EL PASO'S DARKEST DAY

Chapter 11

It was a sunny day when "the Boys" got together for our regular hangout. We kept in touch by meeting up at one of our houses at least once a year. We had to keep the gang together! This month we were riding horses at one of the guys' ranch. The guys and I used to ride motorcycles together, but we have all since given up our motorcycles and swapped them out for horses instead.

After we all had a good, long ride in the desert, we put the horses up and started to get ready to have a cookout. We regularly hung out to catch up and make sure that we stayed in touch with each other's lives, but today was different. Some time had passed since all the chaos our city had gone through. Nobody knew what the other was thinking since the shooting. We all knew we each had been affected in some way, but we didn't know-how. It wasn't a surprise that the conversation turned to guns and mass murders - two things that had saturated most people in our community's everyday chitchat since the shooting.

We initially reminisced about old times. We talked about how we used to go shoot ducks in the Hatch Valley by the river. When we were young guns weren't a big issue and we had always had them in our homes.

"Remember how my grandfather, Jose, had always had a nine-gauge shotgun by his side, I think until he reached about eighty years old?"

"Oh yeah! Of course!" they all yelled in unison. All our cousins and friends growing up knew about my grandpa's doorbell.

If you went to ring the doorbell after sundown, he would pull out his shotgun and point it towards the door and yell, "Who's there!" with the shotgun locked and loaded. After he'd verify it was somebody familiar, he'd put the shotgun down, take out his handkerchief, and wipe off the lenses of his glasses.

"Remember the day Maribel and Dave decided that we should go see for ourselves?" I asked.

"Yeah, man. Of course, I remember," Poncho replied. We all started cracking up as we remembered sitting around, as just teenagers, and talking about what happened right after we'd gotten back that very night.

***

Maribel, Dave, and I waited until sundown. We then jumped in Maribel's car and headed over to where Grandpa Jose's house was in Sunset Heights. Maribel parked the car down the street so he wouldn't be able to tell it was someone he knew. Yes, I know. This was not a good idea.

We waited until it got dark and then crept over to the front porch. Dave and Maribel went up on the porch to ring Grandpa's doorbell. I decided to hang back. I may have been having some concerns about whether this was a good idea. Maribel pushed the button without hesitation: *Ding-Dong*! Sure enough, you could see my grandpa was marching up with his shotgun propped against his right shoulder, aimed right toward the front door.

"Who is it!" he yelled.

"*Abuelo,* it's us, it's us!!!" we all yelled and reached our hands as high as we could.

We had never had a gun pointed right at us. We were frozen like statues. Something about that barrel pointed at you instantly makes you face your mortality. The adolescent sense of invincibility evaporated. We were immobilized in fear for a few seconds.

"You're going to kill someone with that thing! Put it away!" Grandma yelled at Grandpa. He put his shotgun away, and then he proceeded to clean his glasses with his handkerchief.

"We need protection! In Marfa we had no police," Grandpa replied.

"How many times do I have to tell you? We aren't in a ranch! We are in the city! Come in kids," she said and opened the door. Well, we then confirmed that the stories were true. My grandpa was, in fact, *a true ranchero*.

***

My buddies and I laughed as we remembered that day. This led to us talking more about gun control. It had become the constant focus of the media and politicians, post-shooting. This was of course because it

157

was the general public's most outspoken concern in response to the shooting.

I was convinced that good people with background checks should carry guns to protect their own lives. I talked about how our pastor always carried a gun in her purse while she gave her sermons. My cousins in Arizona have always packed a gun, which at the time I thought was a little awkward whenever we would hang out together; however, after all that happened, I could understand it. We all had our own opinions though. One thing that most of us agreed on was that people with gun permits and a good record should be allowed to carry guns if they want too, especially at churches.

"You know, I think that, with proper training, and some gun practice, a person could put a shooter down quickly and efficiently. The shooter always has a blind spot on his back.

All the unarmed people could get down on the ground fast and give anyone with a gun a clear shot. I mean only people that are trained in advance could do something like that. There's too much confusion at the moment. People need to be prepared ahead of time," I said.

"I hear you man," the guys replied.

"I just...I don't ever want our community to be caught off-guard again," I said.

"No. Definitely not," replied George and the other guys nodded.

As the night went on, I started talking about my time as an airman in the United States Air Force. I was a proud soldier. I told the guys about this time I met the president.

"Okay, so I was twenty years old and we were pulling duty at an airbase in Houston for former President George Bush Sr. I was near Air Force One when four Secret Service men drove right in front of me. They, of course, were armed and dressed in black suits, all loaded into the back of an SUV. They pulled up, rolled down the window and ordered, 'Son, go under the president's plane and be sure to protect it from wing to wing!'

"I lit up! I was so excited! 'YES SIR!' I yelled. That day, I would have taken a bullet for him. The president's motorcade began to come towards the plane. A Secret Service guy instructed me to go to some other area, so I was stuck in the back of the hangar. The president was paraded down to his plane and I stood, now way far back, in full salute. As he passed, Barbara Bush noticed me and tapped him on the shoulder and pointed to me. Bush looked over and waved his hand at me. I grinned from ear to ear - beaming with pride."

The guys laughed and teased me about being so innocent. I knew I could protect my church with my training. I know I could have put out that shooter with a few rapid shots.

It was getting late, so we wrapped up and said our goodbyes. It was nice to see the old guys and just have a good time.

While I drove home, I thought about how El Paso has been a relatively safe place. Only an outsider who doesn't know this community could terrorize it like this. To live in El Paso is to love it.

From the first day of the shooting local police departments had been working overtime to create a sense of safety. After the shooting, I got all my kids together and told them that they needed to avoid certain places. I was concerned about the possibility of copycats. I knew it probably wouldn't be in El Paso again because the police are too vigilant, but I didn't care. I needed to keep them safe. The thought of this happening to them because I didn't say or do something kept me up at night.

I arrived home and after tossing my keys on the counter I turned the TV on to wind down. My wife and kids were having a quiet afternoon as I sat down on the couch and turned to the news. It felt like no sooner had I had just warned my kids about copycats than a mass shooting was unfolding in Odessa. I knew there had to be one El Pasoan hurt, and I was right.

The Odessa shooting was too close to home. Many El Pasoans worked in the oil fields in Odessa. Another evil and psychologically disturbed individual shattered the lives of many. A young girl that was just doing her job as a postal worker murdered. I knew what her family was going through. My family and I prayed for God to bless the families and all the victims there, as well as in Ohio.

***

It was a hard year for El Paso, as politicians stigmatized our community with false information. One such false report was that El Pasoans let illegal Mexicans flow freely from the border. There has been a border fence for more than fifteen years here. The illegals that came up to the border fence were being let in with a five-dollar key from Homeland Security. The so-called asylum seekers were mainly Central Americans, and the rest were from all over the world. Immigration officials usually dumped the people in local churches or downtown. Our congregation lost half its members because our church helped Homeland Security with its detainees. Money that our church didn't have was spent on asylum seekers and never reimbursed.

Another piece of false information was that Mexicans were flooding in from the south, when in fact as of 2017 about a little under 75 % of illegal entries were from other parts of the world (Radford and Noe-Bustamante 2019). Hard-working Mexicans like my father that came to this country to work hard and be law-abiding citizens are becoming scarce. Asians are now the highest illegal and legal entries (Radford and Noe-Bustamante 2019).

When you enter our city limits there is a sign that reads: *El Paso an All-American City*. People pay taxes, people are hard workers, and we should be an example of what a successful border city looks like. I have a deed to my house and I pay hefty taxes. This is my home, my land, and my country.

There have been many military families who have been stationed here in El Paso and have decided to make it a permanent home. Fort Bliss has deployed soldiers all over the world to fight against terrorism. To have those soldiers come home and have domestic terrorism on their own soil is downright disgusting.

Thank God for the good people in our town that stepped up to help in every way possible. Let's not forget Angel, from Operation Hope, who was the mediator with the directors at funeral homes, and the mental health that was provided free of charge to whoever needed it. Pastors were calling up families to check on them and the victims, and just to talk. The entire country was very supportive of our community, with emotional and monetary help.

One Fund El Paso raised well over twelve million dollars, which they distributed out to four hundred victims. They used a vetting procedure to dispense the funds. They had strict rules and made the survivors' sign paperwork that involved agreements between families. They were doing a good thing, as they followed the Texas law for disbursement of heirs very strictly - meaning only certain survivors got money. A friend who works at Walmart informed me that the employees that were at the shooting received from nine to ten thousand dollars.

The city of El Paso was instrumental in helping the victims and the community heal. I was surprised at how much the government stepped up to help. The mayor's staff tried to cheer up victims by continuing to invite us to various events. During these outings was when we bonded with the other victims and families and became friends. One of the biggest events was the Khalid concert.

Khalid, who was on a world tour, came to perform in our town. Khalid's performance at the Don Haskins sold out, and he donated his proceeds to the victims. The Khalid family has made many personal donations to the community. What a wonderful family they truly are.

***

As we entered the Don Haskins Center we were blown away by the sheer amount of people not only in the arena but waiting in droves outside to get in. The concert was beyond sold-out. After we scanned into the arena we were ushered to our section where we were sat right next to Khalid's family. My family and I all got to meet and greet Khalid, as well as Matthew McConaughey.

As we were in line to meet Khalid my daughter asked me, "Dad, you're not going to say *Órale* to Khalid, right?"

"No," I replied.

As we walked in I saw Khalid. I outstretched my arms and yelled, "*Órale*! Khalid! Our superstar!"

I turned to my daughter and saw the stunned expression on her face right before she covered her eyes with her hands in shame. Like I could read her mind saying *Dad you didn't just say that!*

"Just because I'm old doesn't mean I don't like Khalid's music! He is the next Juan Gabriel (Mexican international star from the Borderland)."

Khalid laughed, probably at my grin ear -to-ear. My daughter lowered her hands long enough to shake hands with the superstar.

Many other victims and families of victims were there as well. When I noticed Chris Grant, a man that had survived the shooting, I walked over to him to say hi. He had just been released from the hospital with a device still hooked up to his body. He'd always had a good attitude, even just after surviving the shooting. He was walking around in good spirits.

I told him, "Dude! You're the luckiest black man in Texas right now! You look great!"

He laughed. He did look like he'd fully recovered. It was amazing to see.

We talked for a while and he told us, "You know my mother had always carried a gun with her everywhere. Go figure, that one day she forgot to bring it with her. She was all in a hurry thinking she was just picking up a few things."

"Are you all healed up physically?" I asked.

"No," he said and pulled his shirt up while he turned around. You could see a large bandage over his back. He reached around and pulled up the edge exposing the holes from the bullets' exit wounds. They were big and raw. I then knew he still had a long road to recovery. "I have to keep them covered so I don't get it infected, but it's much better."

My niece gave him a gentle hug and told him, "You need to stay home and rest!"

"After Khalid!" he replied. We all agreed. Nobody wanted to miss that concert. It was the first major concert event for us since August 3rd. Plus, it was nice to meet with the other victims. It was great to see everyone healing. All these people that looked like they weren't going to make it, or that were wounded, now were all together with excitement on their faces.

My sister-in-law was with us. She was all excited to meet Matthew McConaughey.

"Oh, I have to meet him, his movies are so awesome!" she said as she beamed while waiting in line to see her favorite movie star. She finally got to the front of the line and took her time talking to Mr. McConaughey - took a picture all excited. He was genuinely nice about it as he has many fans here in El Paso. I'll admit he is a good actor.

We all yelled in unison over each other, "Come, Angie! Let's go! We'll be late to see the concert! We have to get to our seats! Come on!"

When we got to our seat, Khalid's mother was already seated, waiting to watch her son perform. She looked so happy and proud, which she should be. She raised a young man with a huge heart. She did many things right as a mother. Her son turned out to be generous and kind. He raised a huge amount of money for the victims, and he attracted young people out in huge numbers for the event. I've always said that our young people are our future. Khalid set a fine example of the positive impact the youth of our society can have.

Young people in our community were showing their way of healing in their special ways. The school where my kids graduated from, Horizon High School, honored the youngest victim, Javier Rodriguez, a fifteen-year-old. A sunset memorial was held to honor this young man who was just beginning his life. His uncle was shopping with him but survived the shooting. Javier did not.

Jefferson High School students wrote a poetry book in their English class under the guidance of their teacher, Mr. Jim Riddle. Mr. Riddle encouraged his young students to write poetry about this tragic event. I read one poem online and it was amazing the emotion the students had. What a leader to understand his students' need to have an outlet for the complex emotions that the tragedy created.

Another English teacher Mrs. Rebecca N. Guerrero at the Young Women's STEAM Academy participated in the Frontera Rising Project. Amaris Espinoza a ninth grader wrote, "A World I Want to See." This poem is very emotional and describes the feelings through a young student's perspective of the events that shattered our community. I applaud these students and their teachers for using the art of language to heal.

They all let it out through poetry. I've had one or two great English teachers that inspired me to write in the past. I can connect to those students and the work they created. It helped me through this. I advise those students to cherish their teachers.

The healing process was made so much easier with the help of so many that showed sympathy. Whether it was through art or music, people were coming out of the woodwork to demonstrate compassion. El Paso's a town that cares deeply about its people. That's been demonstrated time nd time again during this trauma. I walked out of that concert knowing that it was time to move on. I will just continue to have hope that there will come a time that the shootings end and an era of peace begins.

EL PASO'S DARKEST DAY

Chapter 12

As the healing process moved ahead, I started to process things on a personal level. I was happy for my community. It was great seeing people move on, but I still had a lot of anger. Not in a million years did I think our family would have been involved in such an ordeal. Everyone's seen and heard of the many people who have gone through mass shootings in America, but I still never thought it would be us.

I remember watching news footage of one shooting that stood out to me as being the worst: the Sandy Hook shooting. I was so appalled to see babies shot in a school. My wife is a current teacher and I am a former teacher, so we could imagine what the families had gone through. Now I don't have to imagine. Now I know what it feels like to be the family who is going through having someone take away your loved ones along with your neighbors' and friends' loved ones. All at once – they're gone. Do we just bury people and walk away and just wait for another mass murder to happen? It feels like turning a blind eye to a serious and heinous crime…to just go on with life.

When Maribel's coffin closed I shut my eyes, and I made her a promise. *I will be your voice. I know you would want awareness. I know you would have hope that we could try to prevent these mass murders from ever happening again. I know you would want me to try.*

Many heroes arose in this situation when everything was beyond their control. I hoped those lives didn't die in vain. I want the fallen to be remembered as people who died so others could live. I want everyone to remember that it could have been any one of us shot that day.

Thoughts and prayers came from people around the world. Pope Francis sent blessed rosaries straight from the Vatican to the victims and their surviving families. The city will make a permanent memorial, and hopefully a legacy, to remind us that El Paso prevailed over evil.

One afternoon my niece, Yvette, called me and told me that Stephen F. Austin High School had prepared a memorial for their fallen Panther - Maribel.

I said to her, "Let's go."

Maribel and I had always talked about how our youth are the ones who need guidance. That's the main reason I thought of becoming a teacher. Now the youth was guiding me.

As my wife and I drove toward my old high school to meet up with my niece, I got flashbacks of when Maribel, my brothers, and I attended that high school. I wanted to call Mary and tell her because sometimes my mind didn't register that she was gone. For that moment, I thought that I'd just call up my sister to tell her I thought of her.

We parked and walked up to the gym. The kids from New Tech Sandra Day O'Connor Academy were at the entrance to greet us.

179

Yvette and two of Maribel's grandchildren were there. Dylan was waiting on a front bench and waved at us when we walked in.

"Hey, Al. The students prepared for six months for this celebration ceremony!" Dylan said as he put his arm around my shoulders. "I'll speak first. If you don't mind, can you give a small speech?"

I smiled and nodded and said, "Sure."

Dylan addressed all in attendance. He explained why they were doing the ceremony, and how Maribel had graduated from their school. They had told me I'd be giving a speech about two days prior, so I didn't have too much time to prepare, but I had figured since it was Martin Luther King Jr's Week, I'd tie it to that, and give some history about Austin High School.

As I walked up to the podium to speak, I tried to engage the students by yelling, "Good morning Panthers!!!"

I hadn't been to my old high school in thirty-five years. The gym looked pretty much the same. I stood in front of the microphone, took out my phone where I had my speech, and exhaled.

"My name is Al Hernandez, and I want to thank all of you for making this ceremony possible… to celebrate my sister, Maribel Hernandez. I stand here at this podium at Austin High, looking out at the students. I never thought in a million years I'd be up here giving this type of speech. I didn't think there was going to be so much news media covering this ceremony honoring my sister, Maribel Hernandez."

The crowd looked down intensely at me. I stand here talking about a difficult topic that no one should have to be going through.

"Austin Panthers, how are you guys doing

today? Today we are here, not to talk about tragedy, but about life and healing." "Maribel was a vibrant, young girl full of dreams and hopes, just like many of you young girls present here today. Never in my life did I ever think I would be talking about her here today in this remembrance ceremony. She was a beautiful woman, full of life!

"Maribel had some of the most wonderful moments of her life here. We all had good times together at Austin High School. At two-thirty on Fridays, we'd gather at this gym and have pep rallies with Austin pride before our Friday night football games. Maribel drove us to some of those games. We got to see that big A, that could be seen for many miles, lit up on Friday nights just like you guys. The band would play, and the Panther mascot would dance. But at that time there was something historical happening here at Austin High. In those early years when my sister and I were students something much bigger than any one of us present here, today was happening. You see, in the early years, the country was segregating students by race. Way before even Maribel and I were students, this school was one of the first schools in El Paso, and even the state of Texas, to desegregate.

"Anita Lee Blair was a famous African American that graduated in 1933 from Austin High. I have relatives on my wife's side that were students at Austin High in the fifties and sixties. They described the gradual inclusion of African American students steadily enrolling through the years here at Austin High. Fort Bliss was a major contributor to desegregation because kids from all over the country were bused into Austin High when their parents were transferred to their military base here.

"While Rosa Parks was forced to ride in the back of the bus, African Americans were riding in the front of our school buses. By the time Maribel and I were students here, in the late seventies and early eighties, segregation was gone. We didn't even know what racism was. We had such a diverse student body of all races, and we saw all of each other as Panthers. What our school looked like in the early eighties, most schools didn't look like until quite some time into the future. In the eighties, we mirrored what the country is now beginning to look like, where kids of all races are together. We are all part of a school that is rich in history for a change.

"I remember telling them that we had kids from coast to coast here at Austin High. We didn't have the Internet, so we had to rely on hearsay from White kids from New York. I remember the African American kids in the courtyard with boom boxes dancing and having fun. I told them that we all had one thing in common, and that is that we were all Panthers! What Austin High began is now the aim across the United States.

"Hate is evil, guys. Today we are here to celebrate life! We should remember the fallen at the Cielo Vista Walmart as a beacon of love, hope, and goodness. We need to disarm hate and be kind to one another. We need to show compassion, love, and kindness toward each other. Remember! The definition of evil is the absence of good. The definition of dark is the absence of light. Let's not have hate in our hearts. Let's not remember Maribel and all the others for how they died, but as a beacon of goodness and light! And, when those *candelas* shine bright, we know that we are against all that is evil!

"Now if you are Panthers you remember the four claws and pledge! Repeat after me, Panthers! First claw – don't hate in our school!"

"Second claw – don't hate in our city!"

"Third claw – don't hate in our state!"

"And lastly – "don't hate in our USA!" The students repeated it back and the gym roared with applause. "Thank you all for having us here today and God bless you all!"

In honor of Austin Panther alumna, Maribel Hernández Loya, whose life was taken in a heinous act at Walmart in El Paso on August 3, 2019

"Once a Panther, always a Panther"

The choir band then began to sing a beautiful song. You could tell the students practiced a lot for this occasion. They sang and I could see the tears running down my niece's face. This time her tears were not of sorrow but joy. The students presented us with Maribel's high school picture when she was a freshman there. Maribel's granddaughter, little Desi, was tearful. She witnessed her grandmother's alumni ceremony with the utmost respect.

The Austin jazz band proceeded with a song. I had been a drummer for the band in high school. I loved that part of the ceremony. I could remember how the band used to go all out when we were students, and we'd all be full of pride as the Austin Panther mascot danced to the tunes.

When the jazz band finished, they brought out a mariachi band. A mariachi player asked me, "Sir, we don't know very many songs, but we do know a few. What song would you like us to play?"

"Play the song that reaches your heart, son!"

He nodded and said, "Okay." The Austin mariachi band went all out.

The whole time I had a smile on my face, thinking, "Leo would have loved this mariachi group for sure!" He loved to sing to *Jose Jose Ranchero* in mariachi at our family gatherings and was good at it.

Then a *grupero* group performed who reminded me of the eighties with the song, *Always Together*. Their guitar playing was fantastic, and their vocals were fabulous. I could remember cruising with those, oldies.

In the end, the students presented our family with a plaque. I was amazed at how they could organize this event so well. We were so humbled by their actions of kindness and unity. The plaque still hangs in my mother's living room to this day.

Those students didn't know, but they had put back a part of me that was lost in the shooting. They returned in me a sense that humanity is good. I didn't realize I had lost that until I felt it return. I had lost faith in that at my core. The high school students showed me that, amongst the worst of tragedies good people will bring healing and hope back to you. I hope that the other families of mass shootings can find peace in their hearts again. But I now know it is so much easier when your community comes strong and united. Faith in people has made my life worth living. And that was given back to me.

EL PASO'S DARKEST DAY

Chapter 13

Fiji and my mother became inseparable friends. Fiji has evolved and is now the most obedient dog ever. We can learn a lot from animals. They are so gracious and loyal. She makes my mother laugh when Fiji sees other dogs on television. She'll go up to the screen like she's attempting to reunite with a lost friend. She loves her new home and is now a happy dog.

Healing is sometimes difficult for many that have endured what we have. God heals the brokenhearted and binds up all wounds. Remember that the smallest members of your family look up to you for guidance in difficult times.

This last January was the most beautiful month that I could remember in such a long time. Seasons changed and beautiful sunny days were abundant as I took my family on our road trip. We crossed the Transmountain Road, which was a beautiful sight. On top of the mountain peak, you could see colorful hang gliders in the blue sky. You could see people all along the road enjoying the weather. As I drove up Scenic Drive, it was a clear day and we could see for miles.

Afterward, we decided to go shopping at the Westside. The city was vibrant and full of life. As we went to different stores at the outlet mall, we encountered a store with curios from Mazatlán. Beautiful pottery and art of contemporary Mexico.

The following Sunday I took little Desi, my granddaughter Amy, and my nine-year-old stepdaughter Emily to the *Plaza de Los*

Lagartos. The girls had so much fun running around and just being happy little kids. "Those alligators aren't real, Grandpa?" Amy asked.

"Well, they are."

"No way!" they all yelled at me.

"Okay, they used to be."

"I knew it!" said little Desi.

"You know, when they were real, me and your *Abuela* Maribel used to throw popcorn at them. That was when she was your age, *mijas.*" They looked in disbelief at the statues that remained of the alligators almost as if time just stood still for a moment.

Then my wife and I took them on a streetcar ride. They loved taking the streetcar around downtown El Paso.

"Ahh, nice air conditioning!" I said in relief. The day was hot as the streetcar raced up the hill toward the University of Texas. You could see the city was bustling once again. The restaurants were full, even on a Sunday, and you could see people from Juarez were riding with us.

"Come on guys! Let's get off here," I said and waived the girls toward the door. We got off and bought some ice cream to cool off.

"Hey, let's go to the mountains and hike," I suggested.

"Yeah!" yelled the girls. My wife just smiled. She's always happy if the kids are happy, so off we went!

***

When we stopped at the trailhead parking lot, the kids ran out of the car, teasing each other and laughing.

"Hey, let's go to the place where my father used to take my brothers and sisters and me hiking!" I suggested excitedly.

"Yeah! Let's go!" they of course agreed. If you make anything sound exciting the kids are always on board - especially something new. They're like little explorers.

We climbed up to the same spot that Maribel and I went as kids. The girls were giggling and running around after each other. I looked up toward the mountain, and for a moment, I could see my father taking Maribel, up towards the top of the peak of the mountain. I could see my dad and little Maribel looking back down on us. They were always a step ahead of us.

My dad said to Maribel, "*Sígame, Mija!*" Maribel looked back down at her grandkids, and me, with a sweet smile of delight.

Then little Maribel reached up and said, "Don't leave me Apa!" She took his hand.

"*I'll never let you go, Mija!*" he said as they walked over the summit. She stopped at the top and turned around waving goodbye to us. I stood still, watching as both Maribel and my dad faded, hand in hand…together again, over the top of the mountain.

"Goodbye, my sister. We'll meet again. *Adios!*" I told her. I thought to myself, "I know she followed the light to her home with my dad."

"What *Abuelo*?" Amy asked. I turned to her.

"Oh, just remembering."

"Remembering what?"

"That I love you all so much," I replied and grabbed them all in a big bear hug as they laughed and we all almost fell over. My wife just laughed, and I could see a tear fall from her eyes as one finally fell from mine as well.

EPILOGUE

*As the twenty-third victim Guillermo "Memo"
Garcia just recently died after his nine months
of fighting for his life. He is also an angel and
may he rest in peace.*

*Mr. Mario De Alba is stilling fighting for his life
in his hometown of Chihuahua, Mexico.*

*We have been living through some troubling
times. When the storm subsides, and it will. El
Paso Strong will be revealed once again!*

*May all the victims' families find peace and
healing in their hearts.*

And may God Bless us all so we have happiness once again.

Bibliography

Evans, Robert. "The El Paso Shooting and the
      Gamification of Terror," Bellingcat, August 4,
      2019,
      https://www.bellingcat.com/news/americas/201
      9/08/04/the-el-paso-shooting-and-the-
      gamification-of-terror/

Radford, Jynnah and Luis Noe-Bustamante. "Facts on
      U.S. Immigrants, 2017: Statistical Portrait of the
      Foreign-Born Population in the United States,"
      Pew Research Center, June 3, 2019,
      https://www.pewresearch.org/hispanic/2019/06/
      03/facts-on-u-s-immigrants/

United States Census Bureau. "QuickFacts: El Paso
      County Texas," United States Census Bureau,
      Accessed March 30, 2020,
      https://www.census.gov/quickfacts/elpasocount
      ytexas

AUTHORS PAGE

Al Hernandez is a proud graduate from the University of Texas at El Paso (UTEP) in education. He was a Texas activist who fought against the Sierra Blanca nuclear dumpsite. He continues to reside in El Paso, Texas with his wife and three children.